William Shakespeare's
# Troilus and Cressida
*In Plain and Simple English*

**BookCaps™ Study Guides**
www.bookcaps.com

# Table of Contents

# About This Series

The "Classic Retold" series started as a way of telling classics for the modern reader—being careful to preserve the themes and integrity of the original. Whether you want to understand Shakespeare a little more or are trying to get a better grasps of the Greek classics, there is a book waiting for you!

The series is expanding every month. Visit BookCaps.com to see all the books in the series, and while you are there join the Facebook page, so you are first to know when a new book comes out.

# Characters

PRIAM, King of Troy

His sons:
HECTOR
TROILUS
PARIS
DEIPHOBUS
HELENUS

MARGARELON, a bastard son of Priam

Trojan commanders:
AENEAS
ANTENOR
CALCHAS, a Trojan priest, taking part with the Greeks
PANDARUS, uncle to Cressida
AGAMEMNON, the Greek general
MENELAUS, his brother

Greek commanders:
ACHILLES
AJAX
ULYSSES
NESTOR
DIOMEDES
PATROCLUS
THERSITES, a deformed and scurrilous Greek

ALEXANDER, servant to Cressida

SERVANT to Troilus

SERVANT to Paris

SERVANT to Diomedes

HELEN, wife to Menelaus

ANDROMACHE, wife to Hector

CASSANDRA, daughter to Priam, a prophetess

CRESSIDA, daughter to Calchas

Trojan and Greek Soldiers, and Attendants

**SCENE: Troy and the Greek camp before it**

# Comparable Version

# PROLOGUE TROILUS AND CRESSIDA

In Troy, there lies the scene. From isles of Greece
The princes orgillous, their high blood chaf'd,
Have to the port of Athens sent their ships
Fraught with the ministers and instruments
Of cruel war. Sixty and nine that wore
Their crownets regal from th' Athenian bay
Put forth toward Phrygia; and their vow is made
To ransack Troy, within whose strong immures
The ravish'd Helen, Menelaus' queen,
With wanton Paris sleeps-and that's the quarrel.
To Tenedos they come,
And the deep-drawing barks do there disgorge
Their war-like fraughtage. Now on Dardan plains
The fresh and yet unbruised Greeks do pitch
Their brave pavilions: Priam's six-gated city,
Dardan, and Tymbria, Helias, Chetas, Troien,
And Antenorides, with massy staples
And corresponsive and fulfilling bolts,
Sperr up the sons of Troy.
Now expectation, tickling skittish spirits
On one and other side, Troyan and Greek,
Sets all on hazard-and hither am I come
A Prologue arm'd, but not in confidence
Of author's pen or actor's voice, but suited
In like conditions as our argument,
To tell you, fair beholders, that our play
Leaps o'er the vaunt and firstlings of those broils,
Beginning in the middle; starting thence away,
To what may be digested in a play.
Like or find fault; do as your pleasures are;
Now good or bad, 'tis but the chance of war.

*Troy is where our play starts.From the Greek islands*
*the proud princes, who have been angered,*
*have sent their ships to the port of Athens,*
*full of soldiers and weapons.*
*Sixty nine who wore*
*royal coronets sailed out from the bay of Athens*
*towards Phyriga; they have sworn*
*to destroy Troy, within whose strong walls*

*the kidnapped Helen, queen to Menelaus,*
*sleeps with lustful Paris - and that's what started the argument.*
*They come to Tenedos,*
*and the great ships there unload*
*their military cargo.Now the fresh and yet to be*
*wounded Greeks set up their great tents on*
*the plains of Troy: the six gates of Priam's city,*
*Dardan, and Tymbria, Helias, Chetas, Troien*
*and Antenorides, with great bolts in matching*
*brackets, protect the sons of Troy.*
*Now anticipation stirs up the lively spirits*
*on both sides, Trojan and Greek,*
*putting everything to chance - and I have come here,*
*a Prologue armed not with the weapons*
*of an author's pen or actor's voice but dressed*
*in a costume which suits this story,*
*to tell you, dear audience, that our play*
*skips over the opening skirmishes,*
*beginning in the middle; it starts there,*
*telling everything a play can.*
*Like it or criticise, do as you will;*
*whatever happens, we see it as the fortunes of war.*

# ACT I

# SCENE 1. Troy. Before PRIAM'S palace

Enter TROILUS armed, and PANDARUS

TROILUS.
Call here my varlet; I'll unarm again.
Why should I war without the walls of Troy
That find such cruel battle here within?
Each Troyan that is master of his heart,
Let him to field; Troilus, alas, hath none!

*Call my page here; I'll disarm again.*
*Why should I make war outside the walls of Troy*
*when I have such a battle raging inside me?*
*Every Trojan who is the master of his heart,*
*let him go to battle;Troilus, alas, is not!*

PANDARUS.
Will this gear ne'er be mended?

*Will this business never be straightened out?*

TROILUS.
The Greeks are strong, and skilful to their strength,
Fierce to their skill, and to their fierceness valiant;
But I am weaker than a woman's tear,
Tamer than sleep, fonder than ignorance,
Less valiant than the virgin in the night,
And skilless as unpractis'd infancy.

*The Greeks are strong, with a skill that matches their strength,*
*a fierceness which matches their skill, and a bravery which matches their ferocity;*
*But I am weaker than a woman's tear,*
*softer than sleep, more stupid than ignorance,*
*as timid as a young girl in the night,*
*and as lacking in skill as a child.*

PANDARUS.
Well, I have told you enough of this; for my part,
I'll not meddle nor make no farther. He that will have a cake

out of the wheat must needs tarry the grinding.

*Well, I've spoken to you enough about this; I shall
have nothing more to do with it. Someone who wants
a wheat cake must wait for the wheat to be ground.*

TROILUS.
Have I not tarried?

*Haven't I waited?*

PANDARUS.
Ay, the grinding; but you must tarry the bolting.

*Yes, for the grinding; but you must wait for the flour to be sifted.*

TROILUS.
Have I not tarried?

*Haven't I waited?*

PANDARUS.
Ay, the bolting; but you must tarry the leavening.

*Yes, for the sifting, but you must wait for the dough to rise.*

TROILUS.
Still have I tarried.

*I've still waited.*

PANDARUS.
Ay, to the leavening; but here's yet in the word
'hereafter' the kneading, the making of the cake, the heating
of the oven, and the baking; nay, you must stay the cooling too,
or you may chance to burn your lips.

*Yes, for the rising; but there's plenty that still comes after
that, the kneading, making the cake, heating the oven,
baking; and you must wait for it to cool too,
or you might burn your lips.*

TROILUS.
Patience herself, what goddess e'er she be,

Doth lesser blench at suff'rance than I do.
At Priam's royal table do I sit;
And when fair Cressid comes into my thoughts-
So, traitor, then she comes when she is thence.

*Whatever goddess Patience is,*
*she doesn't suffer like I do.*
*I sit at Priam's royal table;*
*and then fair Cressida comes into my mind -*
*so, traitor to love, she's there even when she's absent.*

PANDARUS.
Well, she look'd yesternight fairer than ever I saw her
look, or any woman else.

*Well, last night she looked more beautiful than I'd ever seen her,*
*and more than any other woman as well.*

TROILUS.
I was about to tell thee: when my heart,
As wedged with a sigh, would rive in twain,
Lest Hector or my father should perceive me,
I have, as when the sun doth light a storm,
Buried this sigh in wrinkle of a smile.
But sorrow that is couch'd in seeming gladness
Is like that mirth fate turns to sudden sadness.

*I was about to tell you:when my heart*
*felt like it would split from sighing,*
*I have covered up the sigh with a smile*
*like when the sun shines in a storm,*
*so that Hector or my father wouldn't notice.*
*But sorrow hidden by faked happiness*
*is like the laughter which fate will suddenly turn to sadness.*

PANDARUS.
An her hair were not somewhat darker than Helen's-well,
go to- there were no more comparison between the women. But, for
my part, she is my kinswoman; I would not, as they term it,
praise her, but I would somebody had heard her talk yesterday, as
I did. I will not dispraise your sister Cassandra's wit; but-

*If her hair wasn't a little darker than Helen's - well, enough*
*of that - nobody would think of comparing them.But, I must say,*

*she is related to me; I don't want people to say I'm biased,*
*but I wish people had heard her her talk yesterday, as I did.*
*I won't put down your sister Cassandra's intelligence; but -*

TROILUS.
O Pandarus! I tell thee, Pandarus-
When I do tell thee there my hopes lie drown'd,
Reply not in how many fathoms deep
They lie indrench'd. I tell thee I am mad
In Cressid's love. Thou answer'st 'She is fair'-
Pourest in the open ulcer of my heart-
Her eyes, her hair, her cheek, her gait, her voice,
Handlest in thy discourse. O, that her hand,
In whose comparison all whites are ink
Writing their own reproach; to whose soft seizure
The cygnet's down is harsh, and spirit of sense
Hard as the palm of ploughman! This thou tell'st me,
As true thou tell'st me, when I say I love her;
But, saying thus, instead of oil and balm,
Thou lay'st in every gash that love hath given me
The knife that made it.

*Oh, Pandarus! I'm telling you, Pandarus -*
*when I tell you that all my hopes are drowned there,*
*don't tell me how many fathoms down*
*they've sunk. I'm telling you that love*
*of Cressida drives me mad. You say, 'She is beautiful'-*
*you push it into my broken heart -*
*her eyes, her hair, her cheek, her gait, her voice,*
*are all subjects of your talk. Oh, her hand*
*which makes all other white seem black,*
*its soft touch makes cygnet's feathers seem harsh,*
*makes the most delicate material*
*as hard as a ploughman's palm! You tell me this,*
*and you speak the truth, when I say I love her;*
*but, when you say this, it's not a sweet medicine,*
*you're twisting the knife of love in the wound.*

PANDARUS.
I speak no more than truth.

*I'm only speaking the truth.*

TROILUS.

Thou dost not speak so much.

*You're not saying half of it.*

PANDARUS.
Faith, I'll not meddle in it. Let her be as she is: if
she be fair, 'tis the better for her; an she be not, she has the
mends in her own hands.

*I swear I won't interfere.Let her be what she is:*
*if she's beautiful, good for her; if she's not, she can*
*make herself so.*

TROILUS.
Good Pandarus! How now, Pandarus!

*Good Pandarus!What do you mean, Pandarus!*

PANDARUS.
I have had my labour for my travail, ill thought on of
her and ill thought on of you; gone between and between, but
small thanks for my labour.

*I've had to work at the job, with both you and her*
*thinking badly of my efforts; I've been the go-between, but*
*got precious little thanks for my efforts.*

TROILUS.
What, art thou angry, Pandarus? What, with me?

*What, are you angry, Pandarus?What, with me?*

PANDARUS.
Because she's kin to me, therefore she's not so fair as
Helen. An she were not kin to me, she would be as fair a Friday
as Helen is on Sunday. But what care I? I care not an she were a
blackamoor; 'tis all one to me.

*Because I'm related to her, I can't say she's as beautiful as Helen.*
*If she wasn't, I'd say I think she's as lovely in her normal clothes*
*as Helen in her Sunday best.But what do I care?I wouldn't care*
*if she was black, it's all the same to me.*

TROILUS.

Say I she is not fair?

*Did I say she isn't beautiful?*

PANDARUS.
I do not care whether you do or no. She's a fool to stay
behind her father. Let her to the Greeks; and so I'll tell her
the next time I see her. For my part, I'll meddle nor make no
more i' th' matter.

*I don't care whether you did or not. She's a fool to stay*
*with her father. Let her go to the Greeks; and that's what I'll tell her*
*the next time I see her. For my part, I'll have nothing more to do with the matter.*

TROILUS.
Pandarus!

*Pandarus!*

PANDARUS.
Not I.

*Not me.*

TROILUS.
Sweet Pandarus!

*Sweet Pandarus!*

PANDARUS.
Pray you, speak no more to me: I will leave all
as I found it, and there an end.
 Exit. Sound alarum

*Please, no longer speak to me: I will leave everything*
*as I found it, and that's the end of it.*

TROILUS.
Peace, you ungracious clamours! Peace, rude sounds!
Fools on both sides! Helen must needs be fair,
When with your blood you daily paint her thus.
I cannot fight upon this argument;
It is too starv'd a subject for my sword.
But Pandarus-O gods, how do you plague me!

———

I cannot come to Cressid but by Pandar;
And he's as tetchy to be woo'd to woo
As she is stubborn-chaste against all suit.
Tell me, Apollo, for thy Daphne's love,
What Cressid is, what Pandar, and what we?
Her bed is India; there she lies, a pearl;
Between our Ilium and where she resides
Let it be call'd the wild and wand'ring flood;
Ourself the merchant, and this sailing Pandar
Our doubtful hope, our convoy, and our bark.
Alarum. Enter AENEAS

*Quiet, you appalling racket! Quiet, vulgar sounds!*
*You're fools on both sides! Helen must be beautiful,*
*for you to be painting her with your blood like this every day.*
*I can't fight for this cause; it's too pathetic an argument for me.*
*But Pandarus–oh gods, how you torture me!*
*I cannot get to Cressida except through Pandarus;*
*and it's as difficult to persuade him to do my wooing*
*as it is to get her to listen to it.*
*Tell me, Apollo, out of your love for Daphne,*
*what is Cressida, what is Pandarus, and what am I?*
*Her home is India; she lies there, a pearl;*
*between our Ilium and her home*
*is the wild and open ocean;*
*I am the trader, and this Pandarus*
*is my uncertain hope, protector and means of access.*

AENEAS.
How now, Prince Troilus! Wherefore not afield?

*Hello there, Prince Troilus! Why are you not at the battle?*

TROILUS.
Because not there. This woman's answer sorts,
For womanish it is to be from thence.
What news, Aeneas, from the field to-day?

*Because I'm not there. This woman's answer is suitable,*
*because not being there is to be like a woman.*
*What happened on the battlefield today, Aeneas?*

AENEAS.
That Paris is returned home, and hurt.

*Paris has come home, wounded.*

TROILUS.
By whom, Aeneas?

*By whom, Aeneas?*

AENEAS.
Troilus, by Menelaus.

*Troilus, by Menelaus.*

TROILUS.
Let Paris bleed: 'tis but a scar to scorn;
Paris is gor'd with Menelaus' horn.
[Alarum]

*Let Paris bleed: he's got what he deserves;*
*he's been wounded by the one he cheated on.*

AENEAS.
Hark what good sport is out of town to-day!

*Hear what good sport there ison the battlefield today!*

TROILUS.
Better at home, if 'would I might' were 'may.'
But to the sport abroad. Are you bound thither?

*There would be better sport at home, if I had my way.*
*But I'll go to the sport outside. Are you going there?*

AENEAS.
In all swift haste.

*As quickly as I can.*

TROILUS.
Come, go we then together.
Exeunt

*Come on then, we'll go together.*

# SCENE 2. Troy. A street

Enter CRESSIDA and her man ALEXANDER

CRESSIDA.
Who were those went by?

*Who were those people who just passed?*

ALEXANDER.
Queen Hecuba and Helen.

*Queen Hecuba and Helen.*

CRESSIDA.
And whither go they?

*And where are they going?*

ALEXANDER.
Up to the eastern tower,
Whose height commands as subject all the vale,
To see the battle. Hector, whose patience
Is as a virtue fix'd, to-day was mov'd.
He chid Andromache, and struck his armourer;
And, like as there were husbandry in war,
Before the sun rose he was harness'd light,
And to the field goes he; where every flower
Did as a prophet weep what it foresaw
In Hector's wrath.

*Up to the eastern tower,*
*where there are views over the whole plain,*
*to see the battle. Hector, whose calm is usually*
*unflappable, was angry today.*
*He scolded Andromache, and hit his armorer;*
*and, showing what a well-organised warrior he is,*
*before the sun rose he had his armour on,*
*and went to the battlefield; every flower there*
*wept like a prophet at what it saw would happen*

*due to Hector's anger.*

CRESSIDA.
What was his cause of anger?

*What caused his anger?*

ALEXANDER.
The noise goes, this: there is among the Greeks
A lord of Troyan blood, nephew to Hector;
They call him Ajax.

*The rumour has it, this: amongst the Greeks there is
a lord of Trojan blood, Hector's nephew;
they call him Ajax.*

CRESSIDA.
Good; and what of him?

*I see; and what about him?*

ALEXANDER.
They say he is a very man per se,
And stands alone.

*They say he's an extraordinary man,
he stands alone.*

CRESSIDA.
So do all men, unless they are drunk, sick, or have no
legs.

*So do all men, unless they are drunk, sick, or have no legs.*

ALEXANDER.
This man, lady, hath robb'd many beasts of their
particular additions: he is as valiant as a lion, churlish as the
bear, slow as the elephant-a man into whom nature hath so crowded
humours that his valour is crush'd into folly, his folly sauced
with discretion. There is no man hath a virtue that he hath not a
glimpse of, nor any man an attaint but he carries some stain of
it; he is melancholy without cause and merry against the hair; he
hath the joints of every thing; but everything so out of joint
that he is a gouty Briareus, many hands and no use, or purblind

Argus, all eyes and no sight.

*This man, lady, has taken on the qualities of many animals:*
*he is as brave as a lion, vicious as a bear, ponderous as an elephant—*
*a man whom nature has filled with so many moods that*
*his bravery has become recklessness, his recklessness touched with*
*discretion. There is no virtue in any man that he hasn't*
*got a bit of, and there's no bad quality missing either;*
*he gets depressed for no reason and is jolly when he shouldn't be;*
*he has all the good parts of men, but strangely put together so that*
*he is like Briareus, with many hands but so full of gout that he can't*
*use them, or shortsighted Argus, with a hundred eyes but still blind.*

CRESSIDA.
But how should this man, that makes me smile, make Hector
angry?

*But why does this man, the sound of whom makes me smile, make Hector*
*angry?*

ALEXANDER.
They say he yesterday cop'd Hector in the battle and
struck him down, the disdain and shame whereof hath ever since
kept Hector fasting and waking.

*They say that yesterday he fought against Hector in the battle and*
*struck him down, which wounded Hector's pride so much that he hasn't*
*eaten or slept since.*

Enter PANDARUS

CRESSIDA.
Who comes here?

*Who's this coming?*

ALEXANDER.
Madam, your uncle Pandarus.

*Madam, your uncle Pandarus.*

CRESSIDA.
Hector's a gallant man.

*Hector's a brave man.*

ALEXANDER.
As may be in the world, lady.

*As much as anyone in the world, lady.*

PANDARUS.
What's that? What's that?

*What's that? What's that?*

CRESSIDA.
Good morrow, uncle Pandarus.

*Good day, uncle Pandarus.*

PANDARUS.
Good morrow, cousin Cressid. What do you talk of?- Good
morrow, Alexander.-How do you, cousin? When were you at Ilium?

*Good day, cousin Cressida. What are you talking about?–*
*Good day, Alexander.–How are you, cousin? When were you at Troy?*

CRESSIDA.
This morning, uncle.

*This morning, uncle.*

PANDARUS.
What were you talking of when I came? Was Hector arm'd
and gone ere you came to Ilium? Helen was not up, was she?

*What were you talking about when I arrived? Was Hector armed*
*and gone before you came to Troy? Helen wasn't up, was she?*

CRESSIDA.
Hector was gone; but Helen was not up.

*Hector was gone; but Helen was not up.*

PANDARUS.
E'en so. Hector was stirring early.

*I see. Hector was up early.*

CRESSIDA.
That were we talking of, and of his anger.

*That's what we were talking about, and about his anger.*

PANDARUS.
Was he angry?

*Was he angry?*

CRESSIDA.
So he says here.

*So this one says.*

PANDARUS.
True, he was so; I know the cause too; he'll lay about
him today, I can tell them that. And there's Troilus will not
come far behind him; let them take heed of Troilus, I can tell
them that too.

*It's true, he was; I know the reason too; he'll do some damage
today, I can tell them that. And Troilus won't be far behind him;
let them look out for Troilus, I can tell them that too.*

CRESSIDA.
What, is he angry too?

*What, is he angry as well?*

PANDARUS.
Who, Troilus? Troilus is the better man of the two.

*Who, Troilus? Troilus is the better man of the two.*

CRESSIDA.
O Jupiter! there's no comparison.

*O Jupiter! There is no comparison.*

PANDARUS.
What, not between Troilus and Hector? Do you know a man

if you see him?

*What, not between Troilus and Hector? Do you recognise a man when you see him?*

CRESSIDA.
Ay, if I ever saw him before and knew him.

*Yes, if I've seen him before and know him.*

PANDARUS.
Well, I say Troilus is Troilus.

*Well, I say Troilus is Troilus.*

CRESSIDA.
Then you say as I say, for I am sure he is not Hector.

*Then you're saying the same as me, for I am sure he is not Hector.*

PANDARUS.
No, nor Hector is not Troilus in some degrees.

*No, and Hector is not Troilus by a long shot.*

CRESSIDA.
'Tis just to each of them: he is himself.

*That's fair to each of them: he is himself.*

PANDARUS.
Himself! Alas, poor Troilus! I would he were!

*Himself! Alas, poor Troilus! I wish he was!*

CRESSIDA.
So he is.

*Well he is.*

PANDARUS.
Condition I had gone barefoot to India!

*That's about as likely as me making a barefoot pilgrimage to India!*

CRESSIDA.
He is not Hector.

*He is not Hector.*

PANDARUS.
Himself! no, he's not himself. Would 'a were himself!
Well, the gods are above; time must friend or end. Well, Troilus,
well! I would my heart were in her body! No, Hector is not a
better man than Troilus.

*Himself! No, he's not himself. I wish he was himself!*
*Well, the gods rule everything; time must make things better or finish them.*
*Well, Troilus, well! I wish my heart was in her body! No, Hector is not a*
*better man than Troilus.*

CRESSIDA.
Excuse me.

*I beg to differ.*

PANDARUS.
He is elder.

*He is older.*

CRESSIDA.
Pardon me, pardon me.

*I can't agree with you.*

PANDARUS.
Th' other's not come to't; you shall tell me another tale
when th' other's come to't. Hector shall not have his wit this
year.

*Troilus isn't fully grown yet; you'll soon change your tune*
*when he is. Hector won't be able to match his intelligence within a year.*

CRESSIDA.
He shall not need it if he have his own.

*He won't need to if he has his own.*

PANDARUS.
Nor his qualities.

*He won't have the same qualities.*

CRESSIDA.
No matter.

*It doesn't matter.*

PANDARUS.
Nor his beauty.

*Nor his beauty.*

CRESSIDA.
'Twould not become him: his own's better.

*It wouldn't suit him: his own is better.*

PANDARUS.
You have no judgment, niece. Helen herself swore th'
other day that Troilus, for a brown favour, for so 'tis, I must
confess- not brown neither-

*You're a poor judge, niece. Helen herself swore the
other day that Troilus, for someone with a dark complexion, which he has,
I must confess–not really dark–*

CRESSIDA.
No, but brown.

*No, it is dark.*

PANDARUS.
Faith, to say truth, brown and not brown.

*I swear, to tell the truth, it's dark and not dark.*

CRESSIDA.
To say the truth, true and not true.

*To tell the truth, it's true and not true.*

PANDARUS.
She prais'd his complexion above Paris.

*She praised his complexion as being better than that of Paris.*

CRESSIDA.
Why, Paris hath colour enough.

*Why, Paris has a good enough colour.*

PANDARUS.
So he has.

*Yes he has.*

CRESSIDA.
Then Troilus should have too much. If she prais'd him
above, his complexion is higher than his; he having colour
enough, and the other higher, is too flaming praise for a good
complexion. I had as lief Helen's golden tongue had commended
Troilus for a copper nose.

*So in that case Troilus has too much. If she praised him above
Paris, then his complexion is redder than his; as Paris has
a good enough colour, and Troilus is redder, then the praise
is no praise at all. It would be just the same as if Helen had
praised him for having a red nose.*

PANDARUS.
I swear to you I think Helen loves him better than Paris.

*I swear to you I think Helen loves him more than Paris.*

CRESSIDA.
Then she's a merry Greek indeed.

*Then she certainly shares out her Greek favours.*

PANDARUS.
Nay, I am sure she does. She came to him th' other day
into the compass'd window-and you know he has not past three or
four hairs on his chin-

*No, I am sure she does. She came to him the other day*
*by the bay window–and you know he hasn't got more than three or four hairs*
*on his chin–*

CRESSIDA.
Indeed a tapster's arithmetic may soon bring his
particulars therein to a total.

*Yes, even a barman could quickly add up*
*his total there.*

PANDARUS.
Why, he is very young, and yet will he within three pound
lift as much as his brother Hector.

*Why, he is very young, yet he can lift weights within three pounds*
*of those his brother Hector can.*

CRESSIDA.
Is he so young a man and so old a lifter?

*Such a young man thrusting so much up?*

PANDARUS.
But to prove to you that Helen loves him: she came and
puts me her white hand to his cloven chin-

*But to prove to you Helen loves him: she came and*
*put her white hand on his split chin–*

CRESSIDA.
Juno have mercy! How came it cloven?

*Juno have mercy! How did it come to be split?*

PANDARUS.
Why, you know, 'tis dimpled. I think his smiling becomes
him better than any man in all Phrygia.

*Well, you know, it is dimpled. I think his smile suits*
*him better than any man in all of Phrygia.*

CRESSIDA.
O, he smiles valiantly!

*Oh, he smiles bravely!*

PANDARUS.
Does he not?

*Doesn't he?*

CRESSIDA.
O yes, an 'twere a cloud in autumn!

*Oh yes, like the sun behind a rain cloud.*

PANDARUS.
Why, go to, then! But to prove to you that Helen loves
Troilus-

*Well, sucks to you, then! But to prove to you that Helen loves
Troilus–*

CRESSIDA.
Troilus will stand to the proof, if you'll prove it so.

*Troilus willbe pleased to accept it, if you can prove it.*

PANDARUS.
Troilus! Why, he esteems her no more than I esteem an
addle egg.

*Troilus! Why, he likes her no more than I like rotten eggs.*

CRESSIDA.
If you love an addle egg as well as you love an idle
head, you would eat chickens i' th' shell.

*If you love rotten eggs as much as you love
empty heads, you will eat half hatched chicks.*

PANDARUS.
I cannot choose but laugh to think how she tickled his
chin. Indeed, she has a marvell's white hand, I must needs
confess.

*I can't help laughing when I think of how she tickled his*

*chin. Indeed, she has a marvellously white hand, I must confess–*

CRESSIDA.
Without the rack.

*And you don't even need to be tortured to do it.*

PANDARUS.
And she takes upon her to spy a white hair on his chin.

*And she said she could see a white hair on his chin.*

CRESSIDA.
Alas, poor chin! Many a wart is richer.

*Alas, poor chin! There are many warts with more hairs on them.*

PANDARUS.
But there was such laughing! Queen Hecuba laugh'd that
her eyes ran over.

*But there was such laughter! Queen Hecuba laughed until
she cried.*

CRESSIDA.
With millstones.

*They can't have been tears of laughter.*

PANDARUS.
And Cassandra laughed.

*And Cassandra laughed.*

CRESSIDA.
But there was a more temperate fire under the pot of her
eyes. Did her eyes run o'er too?

*But the pot of her eyes wasn't boiling over.
Did she weep too?*

PANDARUS.
And Hector laughed.

*And Hector laughed.*

CRESSIDA.
At what was all this laughing?

*What was everyone laughing at?*

PANDARUS.
Marry, at the white hair that Helen spied on Troilus'
chin.

*Why, at the white hair that Helen spotted on Troilus'
chin.*

CRESSIDA.
An't had been a green hair I should have laugh'd too.

*If it had been a green hair I should have laughed as well.*

PANDARUS.
They laugh'd not so much at the hair as at his pretty
answer.

*They weren't laughing so much at the hair as at his clever
answer.*

CRESSIDA.
What was his answer?

*What did he say?*

PANDARUS.
Quoth she 'Here's but two and fifty hairs on your chin,
and one of them is white.'

*She said, 'there are only fifty-two hairs on your chin,
and one of them is white.'*

CRESSIDA.
This is her question.

*That's what she said.*

PANDARUS.

That's true; make no question of that. 'Two and fifty
hairs,' quoth he 'and one white. That white hair is my father,
and all the rest are his sons.' 'Jupiter!' quoth she 'which of
these hairs is Paris my husband?' 'The forked one,' quoth he,
'pluck't out and give it him.' But there was such laughing! and
Helen so blush'd, and Paris so chaf'd; and all the rest so
laugh'd that it pass's.

*That's true; no doubt about that. 'Fifty-two
hairs,' he said, 'and one is white. That white hair is my father,
and the rest are all his sons.' 'By Jupiter!' she said, 'which of
these hairs is my husband Paris?' 'The bent one,' he said,
'pull it out and give it to him.' Everyone laughed so much! And
Helen blushed so much, and Paris was so angry, and everyone else
laughed so much I can hardly describe it.*

CRESSIDA.
So let it now; for it has been a great while going by.

*I wish you wouldn't, you've taken your time over it.*

PANDARUS.
Well, cousin, I told you a thing yesterday; think on't.

*Well, cousin, I said something to you yesterday; do you remember?*

CRESSIDA.
So I do.

*Yes I do.*

PANDARUS.
I'll be sworn 'tis true; he will weep you, and 'twere a
man born in April.

*I'll swear it's true; he will cry for you like the April showers.*

CRESSIDA.
And I'll spring up in his tears, an 'twere a nettle
against May. [Sound a retreat]

*And I'll grow from them, like a nettle
growing in May.*

PANDARUS.
Hark! they are coming from the field. Shall we stand up
here and see them as they pass toward Ilium? Good niece, do,
sweet niece Cressida.

*Listen! They are coming back from the battle. Shall we stand up
hear and see them as they pass on their way to Troy? Good niece, do,
sweet niece Cressida.*

CRESSIDA.
At your pleasure.

*As you wish.*

PANDARUS.
Here, here, here's an excellent place; here we may see
most bravely. I'll tell you them all by their names as they pass
by; but mark Troilus above the rest.

*Here, here is an excellent place; here we can see
very well. I'll tell you who they all are as they pass
by; but look out for Troilus most of all.*

AENEAS passes

CRESSIDA.
Speak not so loud.

*Don't talk so loudly.*

PANDARUS.
That's Aeneas. Is not that a brave man? He's one of the
flowers of Troy, I can tell you. But mark Troilus; you shall see
anon.

*That's Aeneas. Isn't that a great man? He's one of the
greatest in Troy, I can tell you. But look out for Troilus; you shall see
him soon.*

ANTENOR passes

CRESSIDA. Who's that?

*Who's that?*

PANDARUS.
That's Antenor. He has a shrewd wit, I can tell you; and
he's a man good enough; he's one o' th' soundest judgments in
Troy, whosoever, and a proper man of person. When comes Troilus?
I'll show you Troilus anon. If he see me, you shall see him nod
at me.

*That's Antenor. He's a clever fellow, I can tell you; and*
*he's a good man too; one of the best thinkers in*
*Troy, as good as anyone, and a fine figure of a man. When does Troilus come?*
*I'll show you Troilus soon. If he sees me, you shall see him nod*
*to me.*

CRESSIDA.
Will he give you the nod?

*Will he give you the nod? (Slang for "make you a fool" - Ed)*

PANDARUS.
You shall see.

*You shall see.*

CRESSIDA.
If he do, the rich shall have more.

*If he does, you will be even more so.*

HECTOR passes

PANDARUS.
That's Hector, that, that, look you, that; there's a
fellow! Go thy way, Hector! There's a brave man, niece. O brave
Hector! Look how he looks. There's a countenance! Is't not a
brave man?

*That's Hector, there, there, look, there; there's a*
*man! Good for you, Hector! There's a good man, niece. Oh great*
*Hector! Look at his expression. There's a face! Isn't he a*
*great man?*

CRESSIDA.
O, a brave man!

*Oh, a great man!*

PANDARUS.
Is 'a not? It does a man's heart good. Look you what
hacks are on his helmet! Look you yonder, do you see? Look you
there. There's no jesting; there's laying on; take't off who
will, as they say. There be hacks.

*Isn't he just? It does a man's heart good to see him. Look at the
dents on his helmet! Look over there, can you see? Look over
there. That was no play fighting, those were heavy blows,
there's no denying it, as the saying goes. Those are gashes.*

CRESSIDA.
Be those with swords?

*Were they made with swords?*

PANDARUS.
Swords! anything, he cares not; an the devil come to him,
it's all one. By God's lid, it does one's heart good. Yonder
comes Paris, yonder comes Paris.
PARIS passes
Look ye yonder, niece; is't not a gallant man too, is't not? Why, this is brave now. Who said he
came hurt home to-day? He's not hurt. Why, this will do Helen's heart good now, ha! Would I
could see Troilus now! You shall see Troilus anon.

*Swords! It could have been anything, he doesn't care. If the devil came to him it would be the same
to him. By God, it does one's heart good. Here comes Paris, here comes Paris.*
*Paris passes*
*Look over there, niece; that's a brave man too,
isn't it? Well, this is amazing. Who said he came
back wounded today? He's not wounded. Why, Helen will be
pleased with this! I wish I could see Troilus
now! You shall see Troilus soon.*

HELENUS passes

CRESSIDA.
Who's that?

*Who's that?*

PANDARUS.
That's Helenus. I marvel where Troilus is. That's
Helenus. I think he went not forth to-day. That's Helenus.

*That's Helenus. I wonder where Troilus is. That's*
*Helenus. I don't think he went to battle today. That's Helenus.*

CRESSIDA.
Can Helenus fight, uncle?

*Can Helenus fight, uncle?*

PANDARUS.
Helenus! no. Yes, he'll fight indifferent well. I marvel
where Troilus is. Hark! do you not hear the people cry 'Troilus'?
Helenus is a priest.

*Helenus! No—yes he can fight reasonably well.*
*I wonder where Troilus is. Listen, can't you hear the*
*people crying 'Troilus'? Helenus is a priest.*

CRESSIDA.
What sneaking fellow comes yonder?

*Who's that creep over there?*

TROILUS passes

PANDARUS.
Where? yonder? That's Deiphobus. 'Tis Troilus. There's a
man, niece. Hem! Brave Troilus, the prince of chivalry!

*Where, over there? That's Deiphobus. It's Troilus. There's a*
*man, niece. Ahem! Brave Troilus, the Prince of chivalry!*

CRESSIDA.
Peace, for shame, peace!

*Be quiet, you're embarrassing!*

PANDARUS.
Mark him; note him. O brave Troilus! Look well upon him,
niece; look you how his sword is bloodied, and his helm more
hack'd than Hector's; and how he looks, and how he goes! O

---

36

admirable youth! he never saw three and twenty. Go thy way,
Troilus, go thy way. Had I a sister were a grace or a daughter a
goddess, he should take his choice. O admirable man! Paris? Paris
is dirt to him; and, I warrant, Helen, to change, would give an
eye to boot.

*Look at him; make a note of him. O brave Troilus! Look carefully at him,*
*niece; look how his sword is bloodied, and his helmet is more*
*dented than Hector's; look at the way he looks, the way he walks!*
*What a wonderful youth! He is not yet twenty-three. Good for you,*
*Troilus, good for you. If I had a sister or a daughter who were*
*goddesses, he should have his pick. What a wonderful man! Paris? Paris*
*is like dirt to him; and I bet that Helen would give an eye*
*to swap them.*

CRESSIDA.
Here comes more.

*Here come more.*

Common soldiers pass

PANDARUS.
Asses, fools, dolts! chaff and bran, chaff and bran!
porridge after meat! I could live and die in the eyes of Troilus.
Ne'er look, ne'er look; the eagles are gone. Crows and daws,
crows and daws! I had rather be such a man as Troilus than
Agamemnon and all Greece.

*Asses, fools, idiots! Cannon fodder, cannon fodder!*
*Soup after meat! I could live and die in Troilus' company.*
*Don't bother looking, don't bother; the eagles have passed. These are crows*
*and jackdaws! I would rather be a man like Troilus than be*
*Agamemnon and rule all of Greece.*

CRESSIDA.
There is amongst the Greeks Achilles, a better man than
Troilus.

*The Greeks have Achilles, a better man than*
*Troilus.*

PANDARUS.
Achilles? A drayman, a porter, a very camel!

*Achilles? A carter, a servant, an absolute beast!*

CRESSIDA.
Well, well.

*Well, whatever.*

PANDARUS.
Well, well! Why, have you any discretion? Have you any
eyes? Do you know what a man is? Is not birth, beauty, good
shape, discourse, manhood, learning, gentleness, virtue, youth,
liberality, and such like, the spice and salt that season a man?

*Well, whatever! Haven't you any taste?*
*Have you got eyes? Do you know what a man is? Isn't*
*birth, beauty, a good figure, good conversation, manliness, education,*
*gentleness, virtue, youth, generosity and so on the things that*
*go to make a tasty man?*

CRESSIDA.
Ay, a minc'd man; and then to be bak'd with no date in
the pie, for then the man's date is out.

*Yes, a minced up man; one who should be baked without*
*dates, because he's past his sell by date.*

PANDARUS.
You are such a woman! A man knows not at what ward you
lie.

*What a woman you are! Nobody can get past your defences.*

CRESSIDA.
Upon my back, to defend my belly; upon my wit, to defend
my wiles; upon my secrecy, to defend mine honesty; my mask, to
defend my beauty; and you, to defend all these; and at all these
wards I lie at, at a thousand watches.

*I'll lie on my back, to defend my virginity; use my wit to defend*
*my cunning; I'll defend my chastity by protecting my secret places;*
*I'll wear a mask to protect my beauty; and I'll have you to defend*
*everything; I'll keep all these defences around me, for a*
*thousand nights.*

PANDARUS.
Say one of your watches.

*Say what keeps you awake.*

CRESSIDA.
Nay, I'll watch you for that; and that's one of the
chiefest of them too. If I cannot ward what I would not have hit,
I can watch you for telling how I took the blow; unless it swell
past hiding, and then it's past watching.

*No, you can keep awake for that; and that's one of the
chief defences as well. If I can't ward off the attack,
you can make sure fact of it is kept secret; unless
I swell up beyond hiding, and then it will be too late.*

PANDARUS.
You are such another!

*What a woman you are!*

Enter TROILUS' BOY

BOY.
Sir, my lord would instantly speak with you.

*Sir, my lord wants to speak with you at once.*

PANDARUS.
Where?

*Where?*

BOY.
At your own house; there he unarms him.

*At your own house; he's there taking off his armour.*

PANDARUS.
Good boy, tell him I come.
Exit Boy
I doubt he be hurt. Fare ye well, good niece.

*Good boy, tell him I'm coming.*
*I fear he may be wounded. Farewell, good niece.*

CRESSIDA.
Adieu, uncle.

*Goodbye, uncle.*

PANDARUS.
I will be with you, niece, by and by.

*I'll be with you, niece, in a while.*

CRESSIDA.
To bring, uncle?

*Bringing what, uncle?*

PANDARUS.
Ay, a token from Troilus.

*Well, a token from Troilus.*

CRESSIDA.
By the same token, you are a bawd.
Exit PANDARUS
Words, vows, gifts, tears, and love's full sacrifice,
He offers in another's enterprise;
But more in Troilus thousand-fold I see
Than in the glass of Pandar's praise may be,
Yet hold I off. Women are angels, wooing:
Things won are done; joy's soul lies in the doing.
That she belov'd knows nought that knows not this:
Men prize the thing ungain'd more than it is.
That she was never yet that ever knew
Love got so sweet as when desire did sue;
Therefore this maxim out of love I teach:
Achievement is command; ungain'd, beseech.
Then though my heart's content firm love doth bear,
Nothing of that shall from mine eyes appear.
Exit

*By the same token, you are a pimp.*
*In managing someone else's affairs he offers*

40

*words, promises, gifts, tears and everything a lover can offer;*
*but I think a thousand times more of Troilus*
*Than the praises of Pandarus,*
*but I hold back. They think women are angels, when they are wooing them;*
*once they get them that's it; they lose interest after that.*
*If a woman who is loved doesn't know this then she knows nothing:*
*men prefer the things they can't get above those they can.*
*No woman ever got such sweet love from a man who got his desire*
*as she did when he was begging her to grant those desires.*
*So, I take this lesson from the book of love:*
*'when a woman gives in she's under your thumb; if she doesn't you still have to beg.'*
*So, although my heart is full of love,*
*he won't see any of it in my eyes.*

# SCENE 3. The Grecian camp. Before AGAMEMNON'S tent

Sennet. Enter AGAMEMNON, NESTOR, ULYSSES, DIOMEDES, MENELAUS, and others

AGAMEMNON.
Princes,
What grief hath set these jaundies o'er your cheeks?
The ample proposition that hope makes
In all designs begun on earth below
Fails in the promis'd largeness; checks and disasters
Grow in the veins of actions highest rear'd,
As knots, by the conflux of meeting sap,
Infects the sound pine, and diverts his grain
Tortive and errant from his course of growth.
Nor, princes, is it matter new to us
That we come short of our suppose so far
That after seven years' siege yet Troy walls stand;
Sith every action that hath gone before,
Whereof we have record, trial did draw
Bias and thwart, not answering the aim,
And that unbodied figure of the thought
That gave't surmised shape. Why then, you princes,
Do you with cheeks abash'd behold our works
And call them shames, which are, indeed, nought else
But the protractive trials of great Jove
To find persistive constancy in men;
The fineness of which metal is not found
In fortune's love? For then the bold and coward,
The wise and fool, the artist and unread,
The hard and soft, seem all affin'd and kin.
But in the wind and tempest of her frown
Distinction, with a broad and powerful fan,
Puffing at all, winnows the light away;
And what hath mass or matter by itself
Lies rich in virtue and unmingled.

*Princes,*
*what problem has made your faces so long?*
*The great promise that hope offers*
*when we begin our plans on earth*

---

42

*has failed to deliver; stalemates and disasters*
*are blocking our best laid plans,*
*just as knots, getting in the way of the streams of sap,*
*infect the healthy pine, making it grow*
*twisted and away from its natural course.*
*And, Princes, we all know*
*that we have fallen so far short of our expectations*
*that after seven years of siege the walls of Troy still stand;*
*everything we have tried so far*
*of which we have a record has been shown*
*to have gone awry, not fulfilled its purpose,*
*not following the shape of our ideas at all. So why do you Princes*
*look at what we've done shamefacedly*
*and call them failures, when actually all they are*
*are just the long drawn out trials imposed by great Jove*
*to test the persistence of men?*
*That's something which can't be found*
*when dealing with luck; then the brave and the cowardly,*
*the wise man and the fool, the intellectual and the ignorant,*
*the hard and soft, all seem the same.*
*But when distinction frowns and blows upon us*
*with her great powerful fan she blows on all*
*and blows the worthless things away,*
*and things which have a value of their own*
*remain, excellent and unadulterated.*

NESTOR.
With due observance of thy godlike seat,
Great Agamemnon, Nestor shall apply
Thy latest words. In the reproof of chance
Lies the true proof of men. The sea being smooth,
How many shallow bauble boats dare sail
Upon her patient breast, making their way
With those of nobler bulk!
But let the ruffian Boreas once enrage
The gentle Thetis, and anon behold
The strong-ribb'd bark through liquid mountains cut,
Bounding between the two moist elements
Like Perseus' horse. Where's then the saucy boat,
Whose weak untimber'd sides but even now
Co-rivall'd greatness? Either to harbour fled
Or made a toast for Neptune. Even so
Doth valour's show and valour's worth divide
In storms of fortune; for in her ray and brightness

The herd hath more annoyance by the breeze
Than by the tiger; but when the splitting wind
Makes flexible the knees of knotted oaks,
And flies fled under shade-why, then the thing of courage
As rous'd with rage, with rage doth sympathise,
And with an accent tun'd in self-same key
Retorts to chiding fortune.

*With due respect to your divine position,*
*great Agamemnon, Nestor will give proof*
*of what you've just said. Suffering the vagaries of fate*
*shows the true worth of men. When the sea is calm,*
*how many little toy boats dare to sail*
*on her smooth waters, going alongside*
*the great ships!*
*But once the rough north wind stirs up*
*the gentle sea, you'll soon see*
*the well built boat cutting through liquid mountains,*
*leaping between the sea and the sky*
*like Perseus' horse. Then where is the cheeky boat,*
*whose weak poorly built sides a moment ago*
*were matching themselves with the great ones? Either run for the harbour*
*or sunk down to the depths. This is how*
*demonstrations of bravery and real bravery*
*are divided in the storms of fate; when she's shining on people*
*the herd is more annoyed by the breeze*
*than by danger; but when the destructive wind*
*makes the great oaks bend the knee,*
*and the flies flee for shelter–well, then the courageous man*
*become stirred up by the storm, he responds to it,*
*and answers fate in the same way.*

ULYSSES.
Agamemnon,
Thou great commander, nerve and bone of Greece,
Heart of our numbers, soul and only spirit
In whom the tempers and the minds of all
Should be shut up-hear what Ulysses speaks.
Besides the applause and approbation
The which, [To AGAMEMNON] most mighty, for thy place and sway,
[To NESTOR] And, thou most reverend, for thy stretch'd-out life,
I give to both your speeches- which were such
As, Agamemnon every hand of Greece
Should hold up high in brass; and such again

As venerable Nestor, hatch'd in silver,
Should with a bond of air, strong as the axle-tree
On which heaven rides, knit all the Greekish ears
To his experienc'd tongue-yet let it please both,
Thou great, and wise, to hear Ulysses speak.

*Agamemnon,*
*you great commander, the muscles and bones of Greece,*
*the heart, soul and guiding spirit of our army,*
*in which all of our minds should be content*
*to be absorbed–hear what Ulysses has to say.*
*Apart from the praise and agreement*
*which I give to you [to Agamemnon] great one, for your position and power,*
*[to Nestor] and to you, most respected one, for your long life,*
*for both of your speeches–which were so good*
*that, Agamemnon, they should be shown to everyone as*
*models of eloquence, inscribed on brass;*
*and venerable Nestor, with his silver hair,*
*has taken the air and turned it into something as strong as*
*the axle on which the whole universe turns,*
*convincing all the Greeks with his knowledgeable words–*
*but if you'll allow me, you great one, and you wise one,*
*Ulysses would like to speak.*

AGAMEMNON.
Speak, Prince of Ithaca; and be't of less expect
That matter needless, of importless burden,
Divide thy lips than we are confident,
When rank Thersites opes his mastic jaws,
We shall hear music, wit, and oracle.

*Speak, Prince of Ithaca; it's less likely*
*that you would impose on us with unimportant matters*
*than that we would hear sweet eloquence*
*when the foulmouthed Thersites opens his mouth.*

ULYSSES.
Troy, yet upon his basis, had been down,
And the great Hector's sword had lack'd a master,
But for these instances:
The specialty of rule hath been neglected;
And look how many Grecian tents do stand
Hollow upon this plain, so many hollow factions.
When that the general is not like the hive,

To whom the foragers shall all repair,
What honey is expected? Degree being vizarded,
Th' unworthiest shows as fairly in the mask.
The heavens themselves, the planets, and this centre,
Observe degree, priority, and place,
Insisture, course, proportion, season, form,
Office, and custom, in all line of order;
And therefore is the glorious planet Sol
In noble eminence enthron'd and spher'd
Amidst the other, whose med'cinable eye
Corrects the ill aspects of planets evil,
And posts, like the commandment of a king,
Sans check, to good and bad. But when the planets
In evil mixture to disorder wander,
What plagues and what portents, what mutiny,
What raging of the sea, shaking of earth,
Commotion in the winds! Frights, changes, horrors,
Divert and crack, rend and deracinate,
The unity and married calm of states
Quite from their fixture! O, when degree is shak'd,
Which is the ladder of all high designs,
The enterprise is sick! How could communities,
Degrees in schools, and brotherhoods in cities,
Peaceful commerce from dividable shores,
The primogenity and due of birth,
Prerogative of age, crowns, sceptres, laurels,
But by degree, stand in authentic place?
Take but degree away, untune that string,
And hark what discord follows! Each thing melts
In mere oppugnancy: the bounded waters
Should lift their bosoms higher than the shores,
And make a sop of all this solid globe;
Strength should be lord of imbecility,
And the rude son should strike his father dead;
Force should be right; or, rather, right and wrong-
Between whose endless jar justice resides-
Should lose their names, and so should justice too.
Then everything includes itself in power,
Power into will, will into appetite;
And appetite, an universal wolf,
So doubly seconded with will and power,
Must make perforce an universal prey,
And last eat up himself. Great Agamemnon,
This chaos, when degree is suffocate,

Follows the choking.
And this neglection of degree it is
That by a pace goes backward, with a purpose
It hath to climb. The general's disdain'd
By him one step below, he by the next,
That next by him beneath; so ever step,
Exampl'd by the first pace that is sick
Of his superior, grows to an envious fever
Of pale and bloodless emulation.
And 'tis this fever that keeps Troy on foot,
Not her own sinews. To end a tale of length,
Troy in our weakness stands, not in her strength.

*Troy, which is still standing on its foundations, would have been defeated,*
*and great Hector would be dead, except for these reasons:*
*the principles of good government have been forgotten;*
*look how many Greek tents stand*
*empty on this plain, each one represents a false faction.*
*When the leader is not like the hive*
*to which all the worker bees will return,*
*what honey can result? When everyone wears a mask*
*the lowest looks as good as the highest.*
*The heavens themselves, the planets and this earth,*
*follow rank, priority and position,*
*regularity, direction, proportion, season, form,*
*office and tradition, all according to their rank.*
*And so the glorious planet of the sun is*
*placed on a throne on its noble heights and crowned*
*amongst the others, its healing eye*
*keeps all the planets in alignment*
*and speeds, like the orders of the King,*
*without pause, to good and bad. But when the planets*
*wander into an evil conjunction,*
*what plagues and evil signs, what mutiny,*
*what raging of the sea, shaking of the earth,*
*storms in the winds, terrors, changes, horrors,*
*divide, lead astray, tear up*
*the peace and unity of countries*
*absolutely from their roots! When rank is forgotten,*
*which is the path which leads to all noble things,*
*the business will go badly. How could communities,*
*ranks in universities and guilds in cities,*
*peaceful business between distant countries,*
*the rights of inheritance,*

*respect for age, crowns, sceptres, laurel wreaths,*
*survive without rank?*
*Take rank away,untune the string,*
*and listen to the cacophony which follows. Everything becomes*
*complete conflict. The waters of the sea*
*would rise up higher than the shore*
*and drown the whole world;*
*the stupid could rule through strength alone,*
*and a violent son would strike his father dead;*
*force would be right; actually, right and wrong,*
*which justice weighs in the balance,*
*would be forgotten, and so would justice itself.*
*Thenpower would become everything,*
*power would rule over sense, sense would become self-indulgent;*
*there would be no end to debauchery and greed,*
*and in the end the power would consume itself. Great Agamemnon,*
*this chaos is what happens*
*when rank is forgotten.*
*Forgetting about rank means*
*that when we try to move forward all we do*
*is go backwards. The general is held in contempt*
*by the one a place below him, he by the next, the next*
*by the one beneath him; so each one*
*copies the evils of the one above him,*
*everyone begins to develop*
*a grudge against his superior.*
*This is what has saved Troy,*
*not her own forces. To cut a long story short,*
*Troy has survived due to our weakness, not her strength*

NESTOR.
Most wisely hath Ulysses here discover'd
The fever whereof all our power is sick.

*Ulysses has very wisely described*
*the problem afflicting our army.*

AGAMEMNON.
The nature of the sickness found, Ulysses,
What is the remedy?

*Now you've shown us the problem, Ulysses,*
*what's the solution?*

ULYSSES.
The great Achilles, whom opinion crowns
The sinew and the forehand of our host,
Having his ear full of his airy fame,
Grows dainty of his worth, and in his tent
Lies mocking our designs; with him Patroclus
Upon a lazy bed the livelong day
Breaks scurril jests;
And with ridiculous and awkward action-
Which, slanderer, he imitation calls-
He pageants us. Sometime, great Agamemnon,
Thy topless deputation he puts on;
And like a strutting player whose conceit
Lies in his hamstring, and doth think it rich
To hear the wooden dialogue and sound
'Twixt his stretch'd footing and the scaffoldage-
Such to-be-pitied and o'er-wrested seeming
He acts thy greatness in; and when he speaks
'Tis like a chime a-mending; with terms unsquar'd,
Which, from the tongue of roaring Typhon dropp'd,
Would seem hyperboles. At this fusty stuff
The large Achilles, on his press'd bed lolling,
From his deep chest laughs out a loud applause;
Cries 'Excellent! 'tis Agamemnon just.
Now play me Nestor; hem, and stroke thy beard,
As he being drest to some oration.'
That's done-as near as the extremest ends
Of parallels, as like Vulcan and his wife;
Yet god Achilles still cries 'Excellent!
'Tis Nestor right. Now play him me, Patroclus,
Arming to answer in a night alarm.'
And then, forsooth, the faint defects of age
Must be the scene of mirth: to cough and spit
And, with a palsy-fumbling on his gorget,
Shake in and out the rivet. And at this sport
Sir Valour dies; cries 'O, enough, Patroclus;
Or give me ribs of steel! I shall split all
In pleasure of my spleen.' And in this fashion
All our abilities, gifts, natures, shapes,
Severals and generals of grace exact,
Achievements, plots, orders, preventions,
Excitements to the field or speech for truce,
Success or loss, what is or is not, serves
As stuff for these two to make paradoxes.

The great Achilles, who is generally thought
to be the greatest man in our army,
has been listening to everyone's praise of him,
which has made him vain of his value and he lies
in his tent, mocking our plans. He and Patroclus
while away the day lounging in bed,
making scurrilous jokes,
and with ridiculous and clumsy actions–
which, slanderer, he calls imitation–
he mimics us. Sometimes, great Agamemnon,
he pretends to be you,
and, like a strutting actor, whose wits live in
his thighs, and who thinks it's wonderful
to parade around the stage,
with great exaggeration, completely overblown,
he imitates you; and when he speaks,
it's like an untuned bell, not fitting,
with great roars which would seem excessive
from an earthquake. This dirty business
makes the huge Achilles, lounging on his bed,
give a great laugh from his huge chest,
and he cries, 'Excellent! That's Agamemnon exactly.
Now copy Nestor; cough, and stroke your beard,
as if he was getting ready to speak.'
He does it, and is as similar to his subject
as Vulcan was to his wife;
but this great Achilles still cries, 'excellent!
That's Nestor alright. Now, Patroclus, act him for me,
getting ready to answer a night attack.'
And then in truth, the weaknesses of age
are supposed to be funny; he acts him coughing and spitting,
with his hands shaking as he
puts on his armour. Andthis action
makes the great brave one die laughing; he cries, 'Oh, enough, Patroclus,
or give me ribs of steel! I will burst everything
with my scornful laughter.' And in this manner,
all our abilities, gifts, natures, shapes,
individual and group virtues which are of great merit,
achievements, plots, orders, defences,
calls to action, or speeches for truce,
success or loss, what is or is not, becomes
material for these two to mock.

NESTOR.
And in the imitation of these twain-
Who, as Ulysses says, opinion crowns
With an imperial voice-many are infect.
Ajax is grown self-will'd and bears his head
In such a rein, in full as proud a place
As broad Achilles; keeps his tent like him;
Makes factious feasts; rails on our state of war
Bold as an oracle, and sets Thersites,
A slave whose gall coins slanders like a mint,
To match us in comparisons with dirt,
To weaken and discredit our exposure,
How rank soever rounded in with danger.

*Andin imitation of these two–*
*who, as Ulysses says, general opinion*
*gives absolute authority to–many are infected.*
*Ajax has become wilful and looks down his nose*
*at everyone, he's just as vain about his status*
*as broad chested Achilles; he stays in his tent like him;*
*he holds meals for his faction; he criticises our army,*
*as bold as a priest, and encourages Thersites–*
*a slave whose bile produces slanders endlessly–*
*to make comparisons between us and dirt,*
*to make a mockery of our situation,*
*however dangerous it might be.*

ULYSSES.
They tax our policy and call it cowardice,
Count wisdom as no member of the war,
Forestall prescience, and esteem no act
But that of hand. The still and mental parts
That do contrive how many hands shall strike
When fitness calls them on, and know, by measure
Of their observant toil, the enemies' weight-
Why, this hath not a finger's dignity:
They call this bed-work, mapp'ry, closet-war;
So that the ram that batters down the wall,
For the great swinge and rudeness of his poise,
They place before his hand that made the engine,
Or those that with the fineness of their souls
By reason guide his execution.

*They criticise our policy and call it cowardice,*

*they don't think that intelligence has anything to do with war,*
*they obstruct careful planning, and value no acts*
*except physical ones. The quiet and thinking people,*
*who construct the plans of attack,*
*choosing the right time, who work hard*
*to determine the strength of the enemy–*
*they think this is worth nothing.*
*They call it armchair generalship, mapmaking, theoretical war;*
*so they value the battering ram,*
*with its great power and violence,*
*above the engineer who designed it*
*or the one whose superior intellect*
*decided on the strategy for using it.*

NESTOR.
Let this be granted, and Achilles' horse
Makes many Thetis' sons.
[Tucket]

*If we accept this then Achilles' horse*
*is worth many of him.*

AGAMEMNON.
What trumpet? Look, Menelaus.

*What's that trumpet for? Go and see, Menelaus.*

MENELAUS.
From Troy.

*It's from Troy.*

Enter AENEAS

AGAMEMNON.
What would you fore our tent?

*What you want at our tent?*

AENEAS.
Is this great Agamemnon's tent, I pray you?

*Please tell me, is this the great Agamemnon's tent?*

AGAMEMNON.
Even this.

*It is.*

AENEAS.
May one that is a herald and a prince
Do a fair message to his kingly ears?

*May someone who is a Herald and a prince*
*deliver a courteous message to his royal ears?*

AGAMEMNON.
With surety stronger than Achilles' arm
Fore all the Greekish heads, which with one voice
Call Agamemnon head and general.

*I promise with guarantees stronger than the arm*
*of Achilles when he led the Greek army, which is unanimous*
*in calling Agamemnon its head and general.*

AENEAS.
Fair leave and large security. How may
A stranger to those most imperial looks
Know them from eyes of other mortals?

*That's kind permission and a solid promise. How can*
*someone who doesn't know what Agamemnon looks like*
*pick him out from amongst the other men?*

AGAMEMNON.
How?

*How?*

AENEAS.
Ay;
I ask, that I might waken reverence,
And bid the cheek be ready with a blush
Modest as Morning when she coldly eyes
The youthful Phoebus.
Which is that god in office, guiding men?
Which is the high and mighty Agamemnon?

*Yes;*
*I'm asking so I can put on a respectful face,*
*and tell my cheeks to be ready, blushing*
*as modestly as morning when she coldly looks*
*at the newly risen sun.*
*Where is that Godly leader, who guides men.*
*Which is the high and mighty Agamemnon?*

AGAMEMNON.
This Troyan scorns us, or the men of Troy
Are ceremonious courtiers.

*This Trojan is mocking us, or the men of Troy*
*are very formal courtiers.*

AENEAS.
Courtiers as free, as debonair, unarm'd,
As bending angels; that's their fame in peace.
But when they would seem soldiers, they have galls,
Good arms, strong joints, true swords; and, Jove's accord,
Nothing so full of heart. But peace, Aeneas,
Peace, Troyan; lay thy finger on thy lips.
The worthiness of praise distains his worth,
If that the prais'd himself bring the praise forth;
But what the repining enemy commends,
That breath fame blows; that praise, sole pure, transcends.

*Courtiers as noble, gracious, when they are unarmed,*
*as bowing angels–they are well known for that in peacetime.*
*But when they become soldiers, they react to insults,*
*they have good arms, strong joints, true swords and- God willing–*
*unequalled courage. But quiet, Aeneas,*
*quiet, Trojan; stop talking!*
*Praise is worth nothing*
*when it is self praise.*
*When the beaten enemy praises you,*
*that is real praise, pure and transcendent.*

AGAMEMNON.
Sir, you of Troy, call you yourself Aeneas?

*Sir, you man of Troy, do you call yourself Aeneas?*

AENEAS.

Ay, Greek, that is my name.

*Yes, Greek, that is my name.*

AGAMEMNON.
What's your affair, I pray you?

*And what you want, may I ask?*

AENEAS.
Sir, pardon; 'tis for Agamemnon's ears.

*You must excuse me, sir; that's for Agamemnon's ears only.*

AGAMEMNON.
He hears nought privately that comes from Troy.

*He doesn't accept private messages from Troy.*

AENEAS.
Nor I from Troy come not to whisper with him;
I bring a trumpet to awake his ear,
To set his sense on the attentive bent,
And then to speak.

*I haven't come from Troy on a secret mission;*
*I brought a trumpet to tell him I'm here,*
*to get him listening to me,*
*and then to speak.*

AGAMEMNON.
Speak frankly as the wind;
It is not Agamemnon's sleeping hour.
That thou shalt know, Troyan, he is awake,
He tells thee so himself.

*You may speak as freely as the wind;*
*Agamemnon is not asleep.*
*So that you know, Trojan, that he is awake,*
*he's telling you so himself.*

AENEAS.
Trumpet, blow loud,
Send thy brass voice through all these lazy tents;

And every Greek of mettle, let him know
What Troy means fairly shall be spoke aloud.
[Sound trumpet]
We have, great Agamemnon, here in Troy
A prince called Hector-Priam is his father-
Who in this dull and long-continued truce
Is resty grown; he bade me take a trumpet
And to this purpose speak: Kings, princes, lords!
If there be one among the fair'st of Greece
That holds his honour higher than his ease,
That seeks his praise more than he fears his peril,
That knows his valour and knows not his fear,
That loves his mistress more than in confession
With truant vows to her own lips he loves,
And dare avow her beauty and her worth
In other arms than hers-to him this challenge.
Hector, in view of Troyans and of Greeks,
Shall make it good or do his best to do it:
He hath a lady wiser, fairer, truer,
Than ever Greek did couple in his arms;
And will to-morrow with his trumpet call
Mid-way between your tents and walls of Troy
To rouse a Grecian that is true in love.
If any come, Hector shall honour him;
If none, he'll say in Troy, when he retires,
The Grecian dames are sunburnt and not worth
The splinter of a lance. Even so much.

*Trumpet, blow loud,*
*send your brassy voice through all these sleeping tents;*
*and let every Greek of spirit know*
*that Troy wants to announce her intentions.*
*Great Agamemnon, here in Troy we have*
*a prince called Hector–Priam is his father–*
*who has become bored with this dull and*
*perpetual truce. He told me to take a trumpet,*
*and say these words: "kings, princes, lords,*
*if there is anyone amongst the highest of the Greeks*
*who thinks more of his honour than an easy life,*
*who looks for praise more than he fears danger,*
*who uses his bravery and never acknowledges fear,*
*who shows his love for his mistress*
*by performing feats of arms rather than*
*just making her empty promises; I give him this challenge:*

*Hector, in front of Trojans and of Greeks,*
*will prove, or do his best to do so,*
*he has a lady who is wiser,fairer and truer*
*than any Greek ever held in his arms;*
*tomorrow he will blow his trumpet,*
*halfway between your tents and the walls of Troy,*
*to summon a Greek who is truly in love.*
*If anyone comes, Hector will take up his challenge;*
*if nobody does, he'll go back toTroy and tell them*
*that Greek women are sunburnt, and not worth*
*fighting over'. That is all.*

AGAMEMNON.
This shall be told our lovers, Lord Aeneas.
If none of them have soul in such a kind,
We left them all at home. But we are soldiers;
And may that soldier a mere recreant prove
That means not, hath not, or is not in love.
If then one is, or hath, or means to be,
That one meets Hector; if none else, I am he.

*We shall tell our men in love this, Lord Aeneas.*
*If none of them want to take up the challenge,*
*you can say we left them all home; we are soldiers,*
*and a soldier is just an ordinary coward*
*if he means not to be, has not been, or is not, in love.*
*So if one is, or has been, or means to be,*
*that one will fight Hector; if no one else will, I'll do it.*

NESTOR.
Tell him of Nestor, one that was a man
When Hector's grandsire suck'd. He is old now;
But if there be not in our Grecian mould
One noble man that hath one spark of fire
To answer for his love, tell him from me
I'll hide my silver beard in a gold beaver,
And in my vantbrace put this wither'd brawn,
And, meeting him, will tell him that my lady
Was fairer than his grandame, and as chaste
As may be in the world. His youth in flood,
I'll prove this truth with my three drops of blood.

*Tell him about Nestor, someone who was a man*
*when Hector's grandfather was a baby. He's old now;*

*but if there is not one man in Greece,*
*one noble man who has a spark of fire,*
*who wants to defend his love, tell him from me,*
*I'll hide my silver beard in a golden helmet*
*and put armour over these withered muscles;*
*and, when I meet him, I will tell him that my lady*
*was more beautiful than his grandmother and as pure*
*as any in the world. He may be in the prime of life,*
*but I'll stake what little blood I have left to prove this.*

AENEAS.
Now heavens forfend such scarcity of youth!

*Heaven forbid that you should have so few young men!*

ULYSSES.
Amen.

*Amen.*

AGAMEMNON.
Fair Lord Aeneas, let me touch your hand;
To our pavilion shall I lead you, first.
Achilles shall have word of this intent;
So shall each lord of Greece, from tent to tent.
Yourself shall feast with us before you go,
And find the welcome of a noble foe.

*Good Lord Aeneas, let me shake your hand;*
*First of all I shall take you to my tent.*
*Achilles shall be told about this challenge;*
*and every Lord of Greece also, in each tent.*
*You shall eat with us before you go,*
*and accept the welcome due to a noble enemy.*
Exeunt all but ULYSSES and NESTOR

ULYSSES.
Nestor!

*Nestor!*

NESTOR.
What says Ulysses?

*What is it Ulysses?*

ULYSSES.
I have a young conception in my brain;
Be you my time to bring it to some shape.

*I have a plan forming in my brain;*
*help me to get it into shape.*

NESTOR.
What is't?

*What is it?*

ULYSSES.
This 'tis:
Blunt wedges rive hard knots. The seeded pride
That hath to this maturity blown up
In rank Achilles must or now be cropp'd
Or, shedding, breed a nursery of like evil
To overbulk us all.

*It's this:*
*blunt wedges can split tough knots. The pride*
*which has been planted in arrogant Achilles*
*must now be cut down or else*
*it will start to seed, growing a plantation of the same evil*
*which will tower over us all.*

NESTOR.
Well, and how?

*I agree, how will it be done?*

ULYSSES.
This challenge that the gallant Hector sends,
However it is spread in general name,
Relates in purpose only to Achilles.

*This challenge that the gallant Hector has sent,*
*however much it's issued to everyone,*
*it's really only aimed at Achilles.*

NESTOR.

True. The purpose is perspicuous even as substance
Whose grossness little characters sum up;
And, in the publication, make no strain
But that Achilles, were his brain as barren
As banks of Libya-though, Apollo knows,
'Tis dry enough-will with great speed of judgment,
Ay, with celerity, find Hector's purpose
Pointing on him.

*It's true. One can see the purpose*
*in the little details;*
*and when the public announcement is made it's certain*
*that Achilles, even if his brain was as empty*
*as the Libyan Desert–though, Apollo knows,*
*it's empty enough–will quickly come to realise,*
*yes, very swiftly, that Hector's plan*
*is aimed at him.*

ULYSSES.
And wake him to the answer, think you?

*And will he answer the challenge, do you think?*

NESTOR.
Why, 'tis most meet. Who may you else oppose
That can from Hector bring those honours off,
If not Achilles? Though 't be a sportful combat,
Yet in this trial much opinion dwells;
For here the Troyans taste our dear'st repute
With their fin'st palate; and trust to me, Ulysses,
Our imputation shall be oddly pois'd
In this wild action; for the success,
Although particular, shall give a scantling
Of good or bad unto the general;
And in such indexes, although small pricks
To their subsequent volumes, there is seen
The baby figure of the giant mas
Of things to come at large. It is suppos'd
He that meets Hector issues from our choice;
And choice, being mutual act of all our souls,
Makes merit her election, and doth boil,
As 'twere from forth us all, a man distill'd
Out of our virtues; who miscarrying,
What heart receives from hence a conquering part,

To steel a strong opinion to themselves?
Which entertain'd, limbs are his instruments,
In no less working than are swords and bows
Directive by the limbs.

*Yes, it must be him. Who else can you think of*
*who could stand up to Hector,*
*if not Achilles? Although it's not an extreme combat,*
*there is a lot of reputation at stake;*
*the Trojans are putting our reputation*
*to its most extreme test; and trust me, Ulysses,*
*our reputation will be very much at risk*
*in this dangerous business; for success,*
*although it would be in a specific area, will make*
*the people think that we will succeed in the greater battle,*
*and such indicators, although they are very small*
*compare to what comes later, often show*
*in miniature the enormous events*
*which are to come afterwards. It will be thought*
*that the one who challenges Hector is chosen by us;*
*and as we all join together in our choice,*
*the person who goes out to represent us*
*becomes a man representing all our virtues;*
*if he fails, how good it will make the Trojans feel,*
*they will think very well of themselves!*
*When a man feels like this, he fights better,*
*his limbs become his weapons, no less than*
*the swords and bows his limbs employ.*

ULYSSES.
Give pardon to my speech.
Therefore 'tis meet Achilles meet not Hector.
Let us, like merchants, show our foulest wares
And think perchance they'll sell; if not, the lustre
Of the better yet to show shall show the better,
By showing the worst first. Do not consent
That ever Hector and Achilles meet;
For both our honour and our shame in this
Are dogg'd with two strange followers.

*Excuse what I say:*
*so it's best if Achilles doesn't fight Hector.*
*Let's be like shopkeepers, show our worst goods,*
*and see if they will sell; if they don't,*

*the better goods which we've kept back*
*will look even better in comparison. Don't agree*
*to allow Hector and Achilles to ever meet,*
*for whatever happens it looks as though*
*we will come out of it badly.*

NESTOR.
I see them not with my old eyes. What are they?

*I can't see what you mean. What are the bad results?*

ULYSSES.
What glory our Achilles shares from Hector,
Were he not proud, we all should wear with him;
But he already is too insolent;
And it were better parch in Afric sun
Than in the pride and salt scorn of his eyes,
Should he scape Hector fair. If he were foil'd,
Why, then we do our main opinion crush
In taint of our best man. No, make a lott'ry;
And, by device, let blockish Ajax draw
The sort to fight with Hector. Among ourselves
Give him allowance for the better man;
For that will physic the great Myrmidon,
Who broils in loud applause, and make him fall
His crest, that prouder than blue Iris bends.
If the dull brainless Ajax come safe off,
We'll dress him up in voices; if he fail,
Yet go we under our opinion still
That we have better men. But, hit or miss,
Our project's life this shape of sense assumes-
Ajax employ'd plucks down Achilles' plumes.

*Any glory our Achilles gets from Hector,*
*if he wasn't arrogant, we would all share with him.*
*But he is already too proud;*
*it would be more comfortable to burn under the African sun*
*than to face the pride and bitter scorn in his eyes*
*if he beats great Hector. If he is beaten,*
*then we would lose the central pillar of our reputation*
*through the disgrace of our best man. No, we'll have a lottery,*
*and we'll trick blockheaded Ajax into drawing*
*the lot to fight with Hector; amongst ourselves*
*will say that Achilles is the better man,*

---

*for that will please him,*
*he loves to be praised, and he will*
*accept that he is not going to fight.*
*If the dull brainless Ajax comes out safely,*
*we should all applaud him; if he fails,*
*we can still maintain*
*that we have better men. But, win or lose,*
*the success of our projects comes down to this:*
*Ajax must take the place of Achilles.*

NESTOR.
Now, Ulysses, I begin to relish thy advice;
And I will give a taste thereof forthwith
To Agamemnon. Go we to him straight.
Two curs shall tame each other: pride alone
Must tarre the mastiffs on, as 'twere their bone.

*Now, Ulysses, I think this is excellent advice,*
*and I will pass it on at once*
*to Agamemnon. Let's go to him right now.*
*Two dogs will calm each other; they will fight*
*for honour, like two mastiffs with a bone.*
Exeunt

# ACT II

# SCENE 1. The Grecian camp

Enter Ajax and THERSITES

AJAX.
Thersites!

*Thersites!*

THERSITES.
Agamemnon-how if he had boils full, an over, generally?

*Agamemnon–how would it be if he was covered in boils?*

AJAX.
Thersites!

*Thersites!*

THERSITES.
And those boils did run-say so. Did not the general run
then? Were not that a botchy core?

*And those boils started to run, let's say. Wouldn't the general run
then? Wouldn't he lack courage?*

AJAX.
Dog!

*Dog!*

THERSITES.
Then there would come some matter from him;
I see none now.

*Then we'd get something out of him;
we're getting nothing at the moment.*

AJAX.
Thou bitch-wolf's son, canst thou not hear? Feel, then.

[Strikes him.]

*You son of a bitch, are you deaf? Then feel this.*

THERSITES.
The plague of Greece upon thee, thou mongrel beef-witted
lord!

*May a plague of Greece fall on you, you mongrel thick witted
lord!*

AJAX.
Speak, then, thou whinid'st leaven, speak. I will beat thee
into handsomeness.

*Speak then, you mouldy scum, speak. I'll beat you
into decency.*

THERSITES.
I shall sooner rail thee into wit and holiness; but I
think thy horse will sooner con an oration than thou learn a
prayer without book. Thou canst strike, canst thou? A red murrain
o' thy jade's tricks!

*It's more likely that I can abuse you into being intelligent and pious;
but I think it's more likely for your horse to learn a speech
than for you to learn a prayer by heart. You'll hit me will you?
A plague on your stroppy behaviour!*

AJAX.
Toadstool, learn me the proclamation.

*Toadstool, tell me about the proclamation.*

THERSITES.
Dost thou think I have no sense, thou strikest me thus?

*Do you think I have no feelings, striking me like this?*

AJAX.
The proclamation!

*The proclamation!*

THERSITES.
Thou art proclaim'd, a fool, I think.

*You have been proclaimed, a fool, I think.*

AJAX.
Do not, porpentine, do not; my fingers itch.

*Don't push me, porcupine; I'm itching to give you a beating.*

THERSITES.
I would thou didst itch from head to foot and I had the
scratching of thee; I would make thee the loathsomest scab in
Greece. When thou art forth in the incursions, thou strikest as
slow as another.

*I wish you were itching from head to foot and I was
the one to scratch you; I would turn you into the most horrible scab in
Greece. When you go out to battle, you are as slow to strike
as any other.*

AJAX.
I say, the proclamation.

*I'm telling you, I want to hear about the proclamation.*

THERSITES.
Thou grumblest and railest every hour on Achilles; and
thou art as full of envy at his greatness as Cerberus is at
Proserpina's beauty-ay, that thou bark'st at him.

*You grumble and moan all the time about Achilles;
and you envy his greatness just as much as Cerberus envies
Proserpina's beauty–yes, so you bark at him.*

AJAX.
Mistress Thersites!

*Mistress Thersites!*

THERSITES.
Thou shouldst strike him–

*If you hit him–*

AJAX.
Cobloaf!

*You cobloaf!*

THERSITES.
He would pun thee into shivers with his fist, as a
sailor breaks a biscuit.

*He would smash you to smithereens with his fist, like a*
*sailor breaking a biscuit.*

AJAX.
You whoreson cur! [Strikes him]

*You son of a bitch!*

THERSITES.
Do, do.

*Go on, I dare you.*

AJAX.
Thou stool for a witch!

*You witch's toilet!*

THERSITES.
Ay, do, do; thou sodden-witted lord! Thou hast no more
brain than I have in mine elbows; an assinico may tutor thee. You
scurvy valiant ass! Thou art here but to thrash Troyans, and thou
art bought and sold among those of any wit like a barbarian
slave. If thou use to beat me, I will begin at thy heel and tell
what thou art by inches, thou thing of no bowels, thou!

*Yes, do it; you soggy brained lord! You have no more brains*
*than I have in my elbows; an idiot could teach you. You*
*shoddy-brave ass! You're only here to beat the Trojans, you're*
*exploited by those with any intelligence like a barbarian*
*slave. If you're going to beat me, I'll begin at your feet and tell*
*you what you are inch by inch, you gutless object!*

AJAX.

You dog!

*You dog!*

THERSITES.
You scurvy lord!

*You shabby lord!*

AJAX.
You cur! [Strikes him]

*You mongrel!*

THERSITES.
Mars his idiot! Do, rudeness; do, camel; do, do.

*This is the idiot of Mars! Go ahead, rude man, camel; go ahead.*

Enter ACHILLES and PATROCLUS

ACHILLES.
Why, how now, Ajax! Wherefore do you thus?
How now, Thersites! What's the matter, man?

*Hello there, Ajax! Why are you doing this?*
*Hello there, Thersites! What's the matter, man?*

THERSITES.
You see him there, do you?

*You see him there, do you?*

ACHILLES.
Ay; what's the matter?

*Yes; what's the matter?*

THERSITES.
Nay, look upon him.

*No, look at him.*

ACHILLES.

So I do. What's the matter?

*I'm doing so. What's the matter?*

THERSITES.
Nay, but regard him well.

*No, look at him closely.*

ACHILLES.
Well! why, so I do.

*Alright! That's what I'm doing.*

THERSITES.
But yet you look not well upon him; for who some ever
you take him to be, he is Ajax.

*But you're not looking closely at him; whoever
you think is, he is Ajax.*

ACHILLES.
I know that, fool.

*I know that, fool.*

THERSITES.
Ay, but that fool knows not himself.

*Yes, but that fool doesn't know who he is.*

AJAX.
Therefore I beat thee.

*This is what I beat you for.*

THERSITES.
Lo, lo, lo, lo, what modicums of wit he utters! His
evasions have ears thus long. I have bobb'd his brain more than
he has beat my bones. I will buy nine sparrows for a penny, and
his pia mater is not worth the ninth part of a sparrow. This
lord, Achilles, Ajax-who wears his wit in his belly and his guts
in his head-I'll tell you what I say of him.

*Hello hello hello, what specks of wit he comes out with!*
*His attempts are like an ass'. I have beaten his brain more often*
*and he has beaten my body. I can buy nine sparrows for a penny, and*
*his brain isn't worth a ninth of a sparrow. This*
*lord, Achilles, Ajax—who has his brains in his belly and his guts*
*in his head—I'll tell you what I say about him.*

ACHILLES.
What?

*What?*

THERSITES.
I say this Ajax- [AJAX offers to strike him]

*I say this Ajax–*

ACHILLES.
Nay, good Ajax.

*No, good Ajax.*

THERSITES.
Has not so much wit-

*Hasn't got enough brains–*

ACHILLES.
Nay, I must hold you.

*No, I must hold you back.*

THERSITES.
As will stop the eye of Helen's needle, for whom he
comes to fight.

*To block up the eye of Helen's needle, the one he came*
*to fight for.*

ACHILLES.
Peace, fool.

*Quiet, fool.*

THERSITES.
I would have peace and quietness, but the fool will not-
he there; that he; look you there.

*I want peace and quiet, but that fool doesn't–*
*him there; that one; look at him.*

AJAX.
O thou damned cur! I shall-

*Oh you dammed mongrel! I shall–*

ACHILLES.
Will you set your wit to a fool's?

*Are you going to argue with a fool?*

THERSITES.
No, I warrant you, the fool's will shame it.

*No, I bet he won't, because the fool would win.*

PATROCLUS.
Good words, Thersites.

*Well said, Thersites.*

ACHILLES.
What's the quarrel?

*What are you arguing about?*

AJAX.
I bade the vile owl go learn me the tenour of the
proclamation, and he rails upon me.

*I told this wiseacre to go and find out about*
*the proclamation, and he has a go at me.*

THERSITES.
I serve thee not.

*I'm not your servant.*

AJAX.
Well, go to, go to.

*Well, whatever.*

THERSITES.
I serve here voluntary.

*I serve here voluntarily.*

ACHILLES.
Your last service was suff'rance; 'twas not voluntary. No
man is beaten voluntary. Ajax was here the voluntary, and you as
under an impress.

*The beating you just got was suffering; it wasn't voluntary.*
*No man volunteers to be beaten. Ajax was the volunteer,*
*you were conscripted.*

THERSITES.
E'en so; a great deal of your wit too lies in your
sinews, or else there be liars. Hector shall have a great catch
an he knock out either of your brains: 'a were as good crack a
fusty nut with no kernel.

*Exactly; you also have most of your brains in your*
*muscles, if people aren't lying. Hector won't get much*
*if he tries to knock out either of your brains: he might as well crack a*
*rotten nut with no meat.*

ACHILLES.
What, with me too, Thersites?

*That applies to me too, Thersites?*

THERSITES.
There's Ulysses and old Nestor-whose wit was mouldy ere
your grandsires had nails on their toes-yoke you like draught
oxen, and make you plough up the wars.

*There is Ulysses and old Nestor–whose brains*
*were mouldy before your grandfathers were born–they control you*
*like farm animals, and make you slave in their wars.*

ACHILLES.
What, what?

*What, what?*

THERSITES.
Yes, good sooth. To Achilles, to Ajax, to!

*Yes indeed. Yah, Achilles, giddyup Ajax!*

AJAX.
I shall cut out your tongue.

*I shall cut out your tongue.*

THERSITES.
'Tis no matter; I shall speak as much as thou
afterwards.

*It doesn't matter; I'll speak as much sense as you
afterwards.*

PATROCLUS.
No more words, Thersites; peace!

*That's enough from you, Thersites; quiet!*

THERSITES.
I will hold my peace when Achilles' brach bids me, shall
I?

*So I should be quiet when Achilles' tart tells me to?*

ACHILLES.
There's for you, Patroclus.

*He's got you there, Patroclus.*

THERSITES.
I will see you hang'd like clotpoles ere I come any more
to your tents. I will keep where there is wit stirring, and leave
the faction of fools.

*I'll see you hang like the blockheads you are before I come*

74

*back to your tents. I'll stay where there are some brains,*
*and leave this group of fools alone.*

Exit

PATROCLUS.
A good riddance.

*Good riddance.*

ACHILLES.
Marry, this, sir, is proclaim'd through all our host,
That Hector, by the fifth hour of the sun,
Will with a trumpet 'twixt our tents and Troy,
To-morrow morning, call some knight to arms
That hath a stomach; and such a one that dare
Maintain I know not what; 'tis trash. Farewell.

*Now, sir, this is announced through all our army,*
*that Hector, five hours after sunrise,*
*will sound a trumpet betweenour tents and Troy,*
*tomorrow morning, challenging any knight*
*who dares to face him; and anyone that dares*
*say–I don't know what; it's rubbish. Farewell.*

AJAX.
Farewell. Who shall answer him?

*Farewell. Who will fight him?*

ACHILLES.
I know not; 'tis put to lott'ry. Otherwise he knew his
man.

*I don't know; they are drawing lots. Otherwise he knew*
*who he would get.*

AJAX.
O, meaning you! I will go learn more of it.

*Oh, meaning you! I will go and learn more about it.*

Exeunt

## SCENE 2. Troy. PRIAM'S palace

Enter PRIAM, HECTOR, TROILUS, PARIS, and HELENUS

PRIAM.
After so many hours, lives, speeches, spent,
Thus once again says Nestor from the Greeks:
'Deliver Helen, and all damage else-
As honour, loss of time, travail, expense,
Wounds, friends, and what else dear that is consum'd
In hot digestion of this cormorant war-
Shall be struck off.' Hector, what say you to't?

*After the waste of so much time, so many speeches, so many lives,*
*Nestor has once again sent us a message from the Greeks:*
*'Hand over Helen, and all other damages–*
*such as the damage to honour, the loss of time, hardship, expense,*
*wounds, loss of friends, and everything else precious*
*that has been gobbled up in this greedy war–*
*will be written off.' Hector, what do you think of that?*

HECTOR.
Though no man lesser fears the Greeks than I,
As far as toucheth my particular,
Yet, dread Priam,
There is no lady of more softer bowels,
More spongy to suck in the sense of fear,
More ready to cry out 'Who knows what follows?'
Than Hector is. The wound of peace is surety,
Surety secure; but modest doubt is call'd
The beacon of the wise, the tent that searches
To th' bottom of the worst. Let Helen go.
Since the first sword was drawn about this question,
Every tithe soul 'mongst many thousand dismes
Hath been as dear as Helen-I mean, of ours.
If we have lost so many tenths of ours
To guard a thing not ours, nor worth to us,
Had it our name, the value of one ten,
What merit's in that reason which denies
The yielding of her up?

76

*Although no man is less afraid of the Greeks than I,*
*as far as it affects me personally,*
*but, great Priam,*
*there is no lady who has a greater sense of pity,*
*who is more ready to become worried,*
*more ready to cry out, 'who knows what will happen afterwards?'*
*than Hector is. Thegreatest threat to peace is overconfidence*
*and the feeling of safetyit gives; sensible caution is called*
*the guiding light of the wise, the probe that searches*
*until it discovers the worst. Let Helen go.*
*Since this war began on this matter,*
*every soul that war has claimed from us from many thousands*
*was as important as Helen–I meanour men.*
*If we have lost so many lives*
*to guard something that's not ours, and not worth*
*(even if she was Trojan) the value of one soul,*
*how can anybody justify not*
*giving her up?*

TROILUS.
Fie, fie, my brother!
Weigh you the worth and honour of a king,
So great as our dread father's, in a scale
Of common ounces? Will you with counters sum
The past-proportion of his infinite,
And buckle in a waist most fathomless
With spans and inches so diminutive
As fears and reasons? Fie, for godly shame!

*Come, come, my brother!*
*Do you reckon the value and honour of King,*
*as great as our magnificent father, can be measured*
*against ordinary lives? Can you calculate*
*his incalculable greatness with counters,*
*and measure such a great person*
*with such tiny units of measurement*
*as fears and reasons? Shame on you, for God's sake!*

HELENUS.
No marvel though you bite so sharp at reasons,
You are so empty of them. Should not our father
Bear the great sway of his affairs with reasons,
Because your speech hath none that tells him so?

*It's no wonder that you object so much to reason,*
*as you have none of it. Shouldn't our father*
*govern his great affairs with reason,*
*especially as you tell him not to?*

TROILUS.
You are for dreams and slumbers, brother priest;
You fur your gloves with reason. Here are your reasons:
You know an enemy intends you harm;
You know a sword employ'd is perilous,
And reason flies the object of all harm.
Who marvels, then, when Helenus beholds
A Grecian and his sword, if he do set
The very wings of reason to his heels
And fly like chidden Mercury from Jove,
Or like a star disorb'd? Nay, if we talk of reason,
Let's shut our gates and sleep. Manhood and honour
Should have hare hearts, would they but fat their thoughts
With this cramm'd reason. Reason and respect
Make livers pale and lustihood deject.

*You are made for dreams and sleeping, my priestly brother;*
*you make yourself comfortable with reason. Here are your*
*reasons:*
*you know an enemy intends to harm you;*
*you know that swords are dangerous,*
*and reason runs away from anything that can harm it.*
*Is anyone surprised, then, that when Helenus sees*
*a Greek with his sword, he puts*
*the wings of reason on his heels,*
*and flies like scolded Mercury away from Jove,*
*like a shooting star? If we're going to talk about reason,*
*let's close our gates and sleep. Manhood and honour*
*would be as timid as rabbits, if all they fed their thoughts on*
*was this fatty reason; reason and caution*
*make the blood thin and the body weak.*

HECTOR.
Brother, she is not worth what she doth cost
The keeping.

*Brother, she is not worth what it costs us*
*to keep her.*

78

TROILUS.
What's aught but as 'tis valued?

*What's anything worth apart from the value you give it?*

HECTOR.
But value dwells not in particular will:
It holds his estimate and dignity
As well wherein 'tis precious of itself
As in the prizer. 'Tis mad idolatry
To make the service greater than the god;
And the will dotes that is attributive
To what infectiously itself affects,
Without some image of th' affected merit.

*But value can't just be judged by one man:*
*it only has a true worth when it*
*has some intrinsic value, as well as*
*being valued in someone's opinion. It's mad idolatry*
*to value the worship more than the god;*
*and a person is besotted if he attaches himself*
*to something which actually does him harm*
*and has no demonstrable merit.*

TROILUS.
I take to-day a wife, and my election
Is led on in the conduct of my will;
My will enkindled by mine eyes and ears,
Two traded pilots 'twixt the dangerous shores
Of will and judgment: how may I avoid,
Although my will distaste what it elected,
The wife I chose? There can be no evasion
To blench from this and to stand firm by honour.
We turn not back the silks upon the merchant
When we have soil'd them; nor the remainder viands
We do not throw in unrespective sieve,
Because we now are full. It was thought meet
Paris should do some vengeance on the Greeks;
Your breath with full consent bellied his sails;
The seas and winds, old wranglers, took a truce,
And did him service. He touch'd the ports desir'd;
And for an old aunt whom the Greeks held captive
He brought a Grecian queen, whose youth and freshness

Wrinkles Apollo's, and makes stale the morning.
Why keep we her? The Grecians keep our aunt.
Is she worth keeping? Why, she is a pearl
Whose price hath launch'd above a thousand ships,
And turn'd crown'd kings to merchants.
If you'll avouch 'twas wisdom Paris went-
As you must needs, for you all cried 'Go, go'-
If you'll confess he brought home worthy prize-
As you must needs, for you all clapp'd your hands,
And cried 'Inestimable!' -why do you now
The issue of your proper wisdoms rate,
And do a deed that never fortune did-
Beggar the estimation which you priz'd
Richer than sea and land? O theft most base,
That we have stol'n what we do fear to keep!
But thieves unworthy of a thing so stol'n
That in their country did them that disgrace
We fear to warrant in our native place!

*If I get married today, and my choice of wife*
*is made under the supervision of my will,*
*my will inspired by my eyes and ears,*
*two skilful mediators between the dangerous extremes*
*of will and judgement. How can I get rid of,*
*even if my will comes to dislike what it chose,*
*the wife I selected? There is no way*
*to dodge around this and to retain one's honour.*
*We can't return silk to the store keeper*
*when we have soiled it; nor do we throw leftover food*
*into the bin without seeing what can be saved,*
*just because we are full. It was thought fitting*
*for Paris to take some revenge on the Greeks.*
*His sails were blown along by the breath of your agreement;*
*the sea and winds, which usually fight, declared a truce,*
*and helped him; he landed at the ports he had chosen;*
*and in return for an old aunt whom the Greeks held captive*
*he got a Greek queen, whose youth and freshness*
*make Apollo look old and wrinkled, and makes the dawn look dull.*
*Why do we keep her? The Greeks keep our aunt.*
*Is she worth keeping? Why, she is a pearl*
*whose price has launched a thousand ships*
*and made royal Kings into merchants, wanting to buy her.*
*If you agree that it was right for Paris to go—*
*as you have to, for you all encouraged him;*

*if you will admit he brought home a great prize–*
*as you must, for youall clapped your hands*
*and cried, 'incomparable!'–Why do you now*
*criticise the result of your own wise decisions*
*and do something that even Fortune never did,*
*claim that what you once prized more than anything on earth*
*is now worthless? What a disgraceful theft,*
*to steal something and then be afraid to keep it!*
*We are thieves who don't deserve the thing we stole,*
*because we insulted them in their own country,*
*and now we're afraid to justify it when we're on home soil!*

CASSANDRA.
[Within] Cry, Troyans, cry.

*Cry, Trojans, cry.*

PRIAM.
What noise, what shriek is this?

*What's that noise, that shrieking?*

TROILUS.
'Tis our mad sister; I do know her voice.

*It's our mad sister; I know her voice.*

CASSANDRA.
[Within] Cry, Troyans.

*Cry, Trojans.*

HECTOR.
It is Cassandra.

*It is Cassandra.*

Enter CASSANDRA, raving

CASSANDRA.
Cry, Troyans, cry. Lend me ten thousand eyes,
And I will fill them with prophetic tears.

*Cry, Trojans, cry. Lend me ten thousand eyes*

*and I will make them weep for what is to come.*

HECTOR.
Peace, sister, peace.

*Quiet, sister, calm down.*

CASSANDRA.
Virgins and boys, mid-age and wrinkled eld,
Soft infancy, that nothing canst but cry,
Add to my clamours. Let us pay betimes
A moiety of that mass of moan to come.
Cry, Troyans, cry. Practise your eyes with tears.
Troy must not be, nor goodly Ilion stand;
Our firebrand brother, Paris, burns us all.
Cry, Troyans, cry, A Helen and a woe!
Cry, cry. Troy burns, or else let Helen go.
Exit

*Virgins and boys, the middle-aged and the wrinkled old,*
*sweet babies, that can do nothing but cry,*
*add to my noise! Let's pay in advance*
*a part of all the moaning that is to come.*
*Cry, Trojans, cry! Use your eyes for tears!*
*Troy cannot last, or sweet Ilium either;*
*our firebrand brother Paris will burn us all.*
*Cry, Trojans, cry! Helen comes with sorrow!*
*Cry, cry! If you don't let Helen go, Troy will burn.*

HECTOR.
Now, youthful Troilus, do not these high strains
Of divination in our sister work
Some touches of remorse, or is your blood
So madly hot that no discourse of reason,
Nor fear of bad success in a bad cause,
Can qualify the same?

*Now, young Troilus, don't these great words*
*of prophecy from our sister give you*
*some cause for remorse, or are you so*
*hotheaded that no talk of reason,*
*nor fear of a bad outcome in a bad cause,*
*can calm you down?*

TROILUS.
Why, brother Hector,
We may not think the justness of each act
Such and no other than event doth form it;
Nor once deject the courage of our minds
Because Cassandra's mad. Her brain-sick raptures
Cannot distaste the goodness of a quarrel
Which hath our several honours all engag'd
To make it gracious. For my private part,
I am no more touch'd than all Priam's sons;
And Jove forbid there should be done amongst us
Such things as might offend the weakest spleen
To fight for and maintain.

*Why, brother Hector,*
*we can't judge everything*
*only by the way things turn out;*
*neither should we lessen our courage*
*because Cassandra's mad. Her insane visions*
*can't take away the justice of this argument*
*to which we have all committed our honour*
*to make it righteous. Speaking personally,*
*it affects me no more than it does all of Priam's sons;*
*and Jove forbid that any of us would do anything*
*that would give the least courageous any reason*
*not to fight and support.*

PARIS.
Else might the world convince of levity
As well my undertakings as your counsels;
But I attest the gods, your full consent
Gave wings to my propension, and cut of
All fears attending on so dire a project.
For what, alas, can these my single arms?
What propugnation is in one man's valour
To stand the push and enmity of those
This quarrel would excite? Yet, I protest,
Were I alone to pass the difficulties,
And had as ample power as I have will,
Paris should ne'er retract what he hath done
Nor faint in the pursuit.

*Otherwise the world might accuse us of lacking seriousness,*
*both in my actions and your advice.*

*But I swear to the gods, your full agreement*
*drove me onwards in my endeavours, and took away*
*any worries I had about such a serious project.*
*For, alas, what can these arms of mine accomplish on their own?*
*What protection does one man's bravery give*
*against the attack and hatred of those*
*whom this argument involves? And yet I insist,*
*that if I had to face these difficulties alone*
*and had as much power as I have desire,*
*Paris would never take back what he has done*
*and would never lose heart.*

PRIAM.
Paris, you speak
Like one besotted on your sweet delights.
You have the honey still, but these the gall;
So to be valiant is no praise at all.

*Paris, you speak*
*as one who is obsessed with the joy of what you've got.*
*You still have the sweetness, but these others have the bitterness;*
*so there's no credit to you for your bravery.*

PARIS.
Sir, I propose not merely to myself
The pleasures such a beauty brings with it;
But I would have the soil of her fair rape
Wip'd off in honourable keeping her.
What treason were it to the ransack'd queen,
Disgrace to your great worths, and shame to me,
Now to deliver her possession up
On terms of base compulsion! Can it be
That so degenerate a strain as this
Should once set footing in your generous bosoms?
There's not the meanest spirit on our party
Without a heart to dare or sword to draw
When Helen is defended; nor none so noble
Whose life were ill bestow'd or death unfam'd
Where Helen is the subject. Then, I say,
Well may we fight for her whom we know well
The world's large spaces cannot parallel.

*Sir, I'm not just asking you to think*
*about the pleasures such a beauty brings to me;*

*I want the stain of her kidnapping*
*to be wiped out by honourably keeping her.*
*How disloyal it would be to the stolen queen,*
*what a disgrace to your great reputations, and a shame to me,*
*to now surrender her*
*because we've been dishonourably forced to! Can it be*
*the case that such degenerate thoughts*
*have found a place in your generous hearts?*
*The meanest lowest person on our side*
*will still risk himself and draw his sword*
*to defend Helen; and there is nobody so noble*
*that he would not give his life and be celebrated for it*
*if he fell for Helen. So I say*
*it is right that we, whom we know have no match*
*in the whole world, should fight for her.*

HECTOR.
Paris and Troilus, you have both said well;
And on the cause and question now in hand
Have gloz'd, but superficially; not much
Unlike young men, whom Aristotle thought
Unfit to hear moral philosophy.
The reasons you allege do more conduce
To the hot passion of distemp'red blood
Than to make up a free determination
'Twixt right and wrong; for pleasure and revenge
Have ears more deaf than adders to the voice
Of any true decision. Nature craves
All dues be rend'red to their owners. Now,
What nearer debt in all humanity
Than wife is to the husband? If this law
Of nature be corrupted through affection;
And that great minds, of partial indulgence
To their benumbed wills, resist the same;
There is a law in each well-order'd nation
To curb those raging appetites that are
Most disobedient and refractory.
If Helen, then, be wife to Sparta's king-
As it is known she is-these moral laws
Of nature and of nations speak aloud
To have her back return'd. Thus to persist
In doing wrong extenuates not wrong,
But makes it much more heavy. Hector's opinion
Is this, in way of truth. Yet, ne'er the less,

My spritely brethren, I propend to you
In resolution to keep Helen still;
For 'tis a cause that hath no mean dependence
Upon our joint and several dignities.

*Paris and Troilus, you've both spoken well;*
*and you've given a summary of the matter in hand, though*
*only a superficial one;this is what young men do,*
*that's why Aristotlethought they were*
*not suited to hearing moral philosophy.*
*The reasons you put forward are more influenced*
*by your hotheaded passions than*
*a determination to make a proper choice*
*between right and wrong; desire and revenge*
*are deafer than adders when they hear the voice*
*of unbiased decisions.Nature desires*
*that everything should go to its owners.Now,*
*in all of human life, what is closer*
*than a wife to her husband?If this natural law*
*is corrupted by giving in to passion,*
*so that great minds allow their senseless desires*
*to behave contrary to that law;*
*every civilised country has laws*
*to rein in those raging appetites that are*
 *most disobedient and obstinate.*
*If Helen, then, is the wife of the king of Sparta-*
*as we know she is- the moral laws*
*of nature and of all countries say*
*that she should be given back.To carry on doing wrong*
*does not wipe out the original wrong,*
*but makes it worse.Hector is right*
 *about this.But, nevertheless,*
*my spirited brothers, I propose that we*
*still keep determined hold of Helen;*
*because the matter is very important*
*in relation to all our honours.*

TROILUS.
Why, there you touch'd the life of our design.
Were it not glory that we more affected
Than the performance of our heaving spleens,
I would not wish a drop of Troyan blood
Spent more in her defence. But, worthy Hector,
She is a theme of honour and renown,

A spur to valiant and magnanimous deeds,
Whose present courage may beat down our foes,
And fame in time to come canonize us;
For I presume brave Hector would not lose
So rich advantage of a promis'd glory
As smiles upon the forehead of this action
For the wide world's revenue.

*Well, you've put your finger on the crux of my plan.*
*If we didn't value glory above*
*just taking revenge out of spite,*
*I wouldn't want another drop of Trojan blood*
*to be lost in keeping her. But, good Hector,*
*she is a notable and honourable cause for which to fight,*
*an inspiration for brave and selfless deeds,*
*the courage of which may in the present defeat our enemies,*
*and in time may make us immortal;*
*I assume brave Hector would not sacrifice*
*such a great opportunity for glory*
*as this matter offers,*
*not for all the money in the world.*

HECTOR.
I am yours,
You valiant offspring of great Priamus.
I have a roisting challenge sent amongst
The dull and factious nobles of the Greeks
Will strike amazement to their drowsy spirits.
I was advertis'd their great general slept,
Whilst emulation in the army crept.
This, I presume, will wake him.
Exeunt

*I am with you,*
*you brave son of great Priam.*
*I have sent a boastful challenge to*
*the dull and quarrelling nobles of the Greeks*
*which will certainly astonish their sleepy spirits.*
*I was told that their great general was sleeping,*
*whilst the army had begun to copy him.*
*I assume this will wake him up.*

# SCENE 3. The Grecian camp. Before the tent of ACHILLES

Enter THERSITES, solus

THERSITES.
How now, Thersites! What, lost in the labyrinth of thy fury? Shall the elephant Ajax carry it thus?
He beats me, and I rail at him. O worthy satisfaction! Would it were otherwise: that I could beat
him, whilst he rail'd at me! 'Sfoot, I'll learn to conjure and raise devils, but I'll see some issue of
my spiteful execrations. Then there's Achilles, a rare engineer! If Troy be not taken till these two
undermine it, the walls will stand till they fall of themselves. O thou great thunder-darter of
Olympus, forget that thou art Jove, the king of gods, and, Mercury, lose all the serpentine craft of
thy caduceus, if ye take not that little little less-than-little wit from them that they have! which
short-arm'd ignorance itself knows is so abundant scarce, it will not in circumvention deliver a fly
from a spider without drawing their massy irons and cutting the web. After this, the vengeance on
the whole camp! or, rather, the Neapolitan bone-ache! for that, methinks, is the curse depending on
those that war for a placket. I have said my prayers; and devil Envy say 'Amen.' What ho! my Lord
Achilles!

*What's this, Thersites!What, lost in the*
*maze of your anger?Shall the thick skinned clumsy Ajax have the better of it*
*in this way?He beats me, and I shout at him.Well that's a great comfort!*
*I wish it was different: that I could beat him, whilst he shouted at me!*
*By God, I'll learn magic and summon devils, I'll get some result from my*
*spiteful curses.Then there's Achilles, what a plotter!If Troy*
*can't be beaten until these two defeat her, she'll stand there*
*until her walls crumble and fall by themselves.Oh. you great thunder-*
*thrower on Olympus, forget that you are Jove, the king of*
*gods, and, Mercury, may you lose all the power of your snake-wrapped wand,*
*if you can't deprive these two of what little intelligence they have!*
*Useless ignorance itself can see how stupid they are,*
*they couldn't save a fly from a spider without lugging out their great swords*
*and chopping away at the web.And after that, take revenge*
*on the whole army!Actually, give them all the clap!For that, I think,*
*is the curse that will fall on those who go to war for a bit of skirt.*
*I have said my prayers, and the demon Envy says, "Amen!"*
*Hello there!My lord Achilles!*

Enter PATROCLUS

PATROCLUS.

---

88

Who's there? Thersites! Good Thersites, come in and
rail.

*Who's that? Thersites! Good Thersites, come in and attack us.*

THERSITES.
If I could 'a rememb'red a gilt counterfeit, thou
wouldst not have slipp'd out of my contemplation; but it is no
matter; thyself upon thyself! The common curse of mankind, folly
and ignorance, be thine in great revenue! Heaven bless thee from
a tutor, and discipline come not near thee! Let thy blood be thy
direction till thy death. Then if she that lays thee out says
thou art a fair corse, I'll be sworn and sworn upon't she never
shrouded any but lazars. Amen. Where's Achilles?

*If I could have remembered a worthless fake,*
*I would have included you in my curses. Never mind,*
*just be yourself! May you have a great quantity of*
*the common curse of mankind, stupidity and ignorance!*
*May heaven protect you from teachers, don't let instruction*
*come near you! Let your passions rule over you until you die,*
*then if the woman who prepares you for the grave says*
*that you are a good looking corpse I'll swear to it that she*
*had only ever laid out lepers before. Amen. Where's Achilles?*

PATROCLUS.
What, art thou devout? Wast thou in prayer?

*What, are you pious? Were you praying?*

THERSITES.
Ay, the heavens hear me!

*Yes, may the gods hear me!*

PATROCLUS.
Amen.

*Amen.*

Enter ACHILLES

ACHILLES.
Who's there?

*Who's there?*

PATROCLUS.
Thersites, my lord.

*Thersites, my lord.*

ACHILLES.
Where, where? O, where? Art thou come? Why, my cheese, my digestion, why hast thou not served thyself in to my table so many meals? Come, what's Agamemnon?

*Where, where? Oh, where? Have you come? Why, my after dinner treat, why haven't you appeared at my mealtimes for so long? Come, tell me who Agmemnon is.*

THERSITES.
Thy commander, Achilles. Then tell me, Patroclus, what's Achilles?

*Your commander, Achilles. Then tell me, Patroclus, who is Achilles?*

PATROCLUS.
Thy lord, Thersites. Then tell me, I pray thee, what's Thersites?

*Your lord, Thersites. So tell me, please, who is Thersites?*

THERSITES.
Thy knower, Patroclus. Then tell me, Patroclus, what art thou?

*Someone who knows you, Patroclus. So tell me, Patroclus, who are you?*

PATROCLUS.
Thou must tell that knowest.

*You know me, you say.*

ACHILLES.
O, tell, tell.

*Oh, tell us.*

THERSITES.
I'll decline the whole question. Agamemnon commands
Achilles; Achilles is my lord; I am Patroclus' knower; and
Patroclus is a fool.

*I'll explain the whole question. Agamemnon commands*
*Achilles; Achilles is my lord; I am the one who knows Patroclus; and*
*Patroclus is a fool.*

PATROCLUS.
You rascal!

*You rascal!*

THERSITES.
Peace, fool! I have not done.

*Peace, fool! I haven't finished.*

ACHILLES.
He is a privileg'd man. Proceed, Thersites.

*He is given allowances. Go on, Thersites.*

THERSITES.
Agamemnon is a fool; Achilles is a fool; Thersites is a
fool; and, as aforesaid, Patroclus is a fool.

*Agamemnon is a fool; Achilles is a fool; Thersites is a*
*fool; and, as previously mentioned, Patroclus is a fool.*

ACHILLES.
Derive this; come.

*Come on then, explain this.*

THERSITES.
Agamemnon is a fool to offer to command Achilles;
Achilles is a fool to be commanded of Agamemnon; Thersites is a
fool to serve such a fool; and this Patroclus is a fool positive.

*Agamemnon is a fool to try to command Achilles;*
*Achilles is a fool to be commanded by Agamemnon; Thersites is a*

*fool to serve such a fool; and Patroclus is a fool full stop.*

PATROCLUS.
Why am I a fool?

*Why am I a fool?*

THERSITES.
Make that demand of the Creator. It suffices me thou
art. Look you, who comes here?

*Ask your Creator.It's enough for me to just know that you are.*
*Look, who's this coming?*

ACHILLES.
Come, Patroclus, I'll speak with nobody. Come in with me,
Thersites.
Exit

*Come, Patroclus, I don't want to speak to anybody.*

THERSITES.
Here is such patchery, such juggling, and such knavery.
All the argument is a whore and a cuckold-a good quarrel to draw
emulous factions and bleed to death upon. Now the dry serpigo on
the subject, and war and lechery confound all!
Exit

*There is such stupidity, such trickery and such knavery here.*
*The whole war is about a cuckold and a whore - fine things*
*to split into factions and bleed to death over.A plague on*
*the subject, and may war and their lechery damn them all!*

Enter AGAMEMNON, ULYSSES, NESTOR, DIOMEDES,
AJAX, and CALCHAS

AGAMEMNON.
Where is Achilles?

*Where is Achilles?*

PATROCLUS.
Within his tent; but ill-dispos'd, my lord.

———

*Inside his tent; but not entertaining, my lord.*

AGAMEMNON.
Let it be known to him that we are here.
He shent our messengers; and we lay by
Our appertainings, visiting of him.
Let him be told so; lest, perchance, he think
We dare not move the question of our place
Or know not what we are.

*Let him know that I am here.*
*he insulted my messengers; and I am*
*lowering myself by visiting him.*
*Tell him this, in case he thinks*
*that I won't assert my authority*
*or don't know my position.*

PATROCLUS.
I shall say so to him.
Exit

*I'll tell him.*

ULYSSES.
We saw him at the opening of his tent.
He is not sick.

*I saw him at the entrance to his tent.*
*He's not ill.*

AJAX.
Yes, lion-sick, sick of proud heart. You may call it
melancholy, if you will favour the man; but, by my head, 'tis
pride. But why, why? Let him show us a cause. A word, my lord.
[Takes AGAMEMNON aside]

*He's sick as a lion, sick from pride. You can call it*
*depression, if you're on his side; but to me it is*
*pride. But why, why? Let him show us a reason. A word, my lord.*

NESTOR.
What moves Ajax thus to bay at him?

*What makes Ajax rant at him like that?*

ULYSSES.
Achilles hath inveigled his fool from him.

*Achilles has persuaded his fool away from him.*

NESTOR.
Who, Thersites?

*Who, Thersites?*

ULYSSES.
He.

*Him.*

NESTOR.
Then will Ajax lack matter, if he have lost his argument.

*Then Ajax will have nothing to say, if he's lost the thing he's complaining about.*

ULYSSES.
No; you see he is his argument that has his argument-
Achilles.

*No; you see, the one he wants to argue with is the one who has taken
what he's talking about away - Achilles.*

NESTOR.
All the better; their fraction is more our wish than their
faction. But it was a strong composure a fool could disunite!

*So much the better; we're better off with them divided rather than united
against us.But they hardly had a great bond, if a fool can split them up!*

ULYSSES.
The amity that wisdom knits not, folly may easily untie.

*If a friendship isn't based on wisdom then stupidity can easily break it.*

Re-enter PATROCLUS

Here comes Patroclus.

*Here come Patroclus.*

NESTOR.
No Achilles with him.

*No Achilles with him.*

ULYSSES.
The elephant hath joints, but none for courtesy; his legs
are legs for necessity, not for flexure.

*The elephant has joints, but none to kneel politely;*
*he only has them for necessity, not for showing respect.*

PATROCLUS.
Achilles bids me say he is much sorry
If any thing more than your sport and pleasure
Did move your greatness and this noble state
To call upon him; he hopes it is no other
But for your health and your digestion sake,
An after-dinner's breath.

*Achilles tells me to say that he's very sorry*
*if it was anything more than your fun and pleasure*
*which made your highness and your noble entourage*
*come calling; he hopes you're just out*
*for the sake of your health and digestion,*
*getting a breath of air after dinner.*

AGAMEMNON.
Hear you, Patroclus.
We are too well acquainted with these answers;
But his evasion, wing'd thus swift with scorn,
Cannot outfly our apprehensions.
Much attribute he hath, and much the reason
Why we ascribe it to him. Yet all his virtues,
Not virtuously on his own part beheld,
Do in our eyes begin to lose their gloss;
Yea, like fair fruit in an unwholesome dish,
Are like to rot untasted. Go and tell him
We come to speak with him; and you shall not sin
If you do say we think him over-proud
And under-honest, in self-assumption greater
Than in the note of judgment; and worthier than himself

Here tend the savage strangeness he puts on,
Disguise the holy strength of their command,
And underwrite in an observing kind
His humorous predominance; yea, watch
His pettish lunes, his ebbs, his flows, as if
The passage and whole carriage of this action
Rode on his tide. Go tell him this, and add
That if he overhold his price so much
We'll none of him, but let him, like an engine
Not portable, lie under this report:
Bring action hither; this cannot go to war.
A stirring dwarf we do allowance give
Before a sleeping giant. Tell him so.

*Listen to me, Patroclus.*
*We've had enough of these answers;*
*but his evasions, quick as scorn makes them,*
*can't fool us.*
*He has great honour, and good reasons*
*why we give it to him. But all his virtues,*
*now that he's not living up to them,*
*are starting to look dirty in our eyes;*
*they're like sweet fruit in a dirty dish,*
*they'll rot if they're not tasted. Go and tell him*
*I have come to speak to him; and it will not be a lie*
*if you tell him we think he is too proud*
*and impolite, and that he thinks more of himself*
*than public opinion does; greater people than him*
*are waiting here while he assumes a rude and barbarous aloofness,*
*and they are reining in their holy right to command,*
*and are tolerating whatever mood is dominating him,*
*just watching him; yes, watching*
*his little tantrums, his mood swings, as if*
*the entire outcome of the war*
*depended on him. Go and tell him this, and add*
*that if he thinks he's too good for us*
*we'll have nothing to do with him, and he will*
*be like an siege engine which can't be shifted,*
*and we shall say this of him:*
*"Let's go, this is useless in war."*
*We shall be more favourable to a dwarf who wants to fight*
*than to a sleeping giant. Tell him that.*

PATROCLUS.

———

I shall, and bring his answer presently.
Exit

*I shall, and I'll bring you his answer shortly.*

AGAMEMNON.
In second voice we'll not be satisfied;
We come to speak with him. Ulysses, enter you.

*I'm not being spoken to through an intermediary;*
*I've come to speak to him. Ulysses, go in to his tent.*

Exit ULYSSES

AJAX.
What is he more than another?

*What makes him better than anyone else?*

AGAMEMNON.
No more than what he thinks he is.

*Only his own opinion.*

AJAX.
Is he so much? Do you not think he thinks himself a better
man than I am?

*Is he that great? Do you think that he thinks he's a better*
*man than I am?*

AGAMEMNON.
No question.

*Without question.*

AJAX.
Will you subscribe his thought and say he is?

*Do you agree with him?*

AGAMEMNON.
No, noble Ajax; you are as strong, as valiant, as wise,
no less noble, much more gentle, and altogether more tractable.

*No, noble Ajax; you are just as strong, as brave, as wise,*
*no less noble, much more gentle, and much more obedient.*

AJAX.
Why should a man be proud? How doth pride grow? I know not
what pride is.

*Why should a man be proud? What makes him proud? I don't know*
*what pride is.*

AGAMEMNON.
Your mind is the clearer, Ajax, and your virtues the
fairer. He that is proud eats up himself. Pride is his own glass,
his own trumpet, his own chronicle; and whatever praises itself
but in the deed devours the deed in the praise.

*Your mind is clearer, Ajax, and your virtues are*
*better. The proud man consumes himself. His pride is his own mirror,*
*blows his own trumpet, writes his own praise; and anything that praises*
*itself destroys the good thing it's done by doing so.*

Re-enter ULYSSES

AJAX.
I do hate a proud man as I do hate the engend'ring of toads.

*I hate a proud man just as I hate toad spawn.*

NESTOR.
[Aside] And yet he loves himself: is't not strange?

*And yet he loves himself, isn't that strange?*

ULYSSES.
Achilles will not to the field to-morrow.

*Achilles will not fight tomorrow.*

AGAMEMNON.
What's his excuse?

*What's his excuse?*

ULYSSES.
He doth rely on none;
But carries on the stream of his dispose,
Without observance or respect of any,
In will peculiar and in self-admission.

*He gives none;*
*he's just carrying on as before,*
*taking no notice of, and giving no respect to, anyone else,*
*just following whatever his ego wants.*

AGAMEMNON.
Why will he not, upon our fair request,
Untent his person and share the air with us?

*Why won't he, when we've asked politely,*
*come out of his tent and talk with us?*

ULYSSES.
Things small as nothing, for request's sake only,
He makes important; possess'd he is with greatness,
And speaks not to himself but with a pride
That quarrels at self-breath. Imagin'd worth
Holds in his blood such swol'n and hot discourse
That 'twixt his mental and his active parts
Kingdom'd Achilles in commotion rages,
And batters down himself. What should I say?
He is so plaguy proud that the death tokens of it
Cry 'No recovery.'

*He makes a great issue out of tiny things,*
*just because they've been asked; he's obsessed with his own greatness,*
*and can't even talk to himself without starting*
*an argument.His high opinion of himself*
*has fired him up so much*
*that his mind and body*
*are having a civil war with each other,*
*tearing him to bits.What can I say?*
*He is so plagued with pride that the symptoms*
*of it say he won't recover.*

AGAMEMNON.
Let Ajax go to him.
Dear lord, go you and greet him in his tent.

'Tis said he holds you well; and will be led
At your request a little from himself.

*Let Ajax speak to him.*
*Dear lord, you go and greet him in his tent.*
*They say he thinks well of you; perhaps he'll*
*soften his attitude if you ask him to.*

ULYSSES.
O Agamemnon, let it not be so!
We'll consecrate the steps that Ajax makes
When they go from Achilles. Shall the proud lord
That bastes his arrogance with his own seam
And never suffers matter of the world
Enter his thoughts, save such as doth revolve
And ruminate himself-shall he be worshipp'd
Of that we hold an idol more than he?
No, this thrice-worthy and right valiant lord
Shall not so stale his palm, nobly acquir'd,
Nor, by my will, assubjugate his merit,
As amply titled as Achilles is,
By going to Achilles.
That were to enlard his fat-already pride,
And add more coals to Cancer when he burns
With entertaining great Hyperion.
This lord go to him! Jupiter forbid,
And say in thunder 'Achilles go to him.'

*Oh Agamemnon, don't do this!*
*We'd rather worship Ajax for staying away from*
*Achilles.Should the proud lord*
*who roasts in the fat of his own arrogance*
*and never allows anybody else to*
*enter his thoughts, unless it's some matter*
*which revolves around himself - should someone we think*
*is far greater bow down to him?*
*No, this triply-worthy and truly brave lord*
*shouldn't tarnish his honour, which was bravely won,*
*and I don't want him to debase himself,*
*however great Achilles is,*
*by going to Achilles.*
*That would add more lard to his already greasy pride,*
*and add fire to the heat of summer.*
*To say this lord should go to him!Jupiter forbid,*

and he should thunder out, "Achilles should come to him."

NESTOR.
[Aside] O, this is well! He rubs the vein of him.

*Ah, this is good! He's encouraging what he already thinks.*

DIOMEDES.
[Aside] And how his silence drinks up this applause!

*And how that's shown in his silence!*

AJAX.
If I go to him, with my armed fist I'll pash him o'er the face.

*If I go to see him I'll smash him in the face with my mailed fist.*

AGAMEMNON.
O, no, you shall not go.

*Oh, no, you shan't go.*

AJAX.
An 'a be proud with me I'll pheeze his pride.
Let me go to him.

*And if he starts being arrogant with me I'll sort his pride out.*
*Let me go to him.*

ULYSSES.
Not for the worth that hangs upon our quarrel.

*Not for everything we've spent on this war.*

AJAX.
A paltry, insolent fellow!

*A shabby, insolent fellow!*

NESTOR.
[Aside] How he describes himself!

*He's describing himself!*

AJAX.
Can he not be sociable?

*Can't he be friendly?*

ULYSSES.
[Aside] The raven chides blackness.

*The pot calls the kettle black.*

AJAX.
I'll let his humours blood.

*I'll treat his moods with a bloodletting.*

AGAMEMNON.
[Aside] He will be the physician that should be the
patient.

*He wants to be the doctor when he should be the patient.*

AJAX.
An all men were a my mind-

*If all men thought like me-*

ULYSSES.
[Aside] Wit would be out of fashion.

*There's be no brains anywhere.*

AJAX.
'A should not bear it so, 'a should eat swords first.
Shall pride carry it?

*He wouldn't get away with this, he would eat my sword first.*
*Should pride get away with this?*

NESTOR.
[Aside] An 'twould, you'd carry half.

*If it did, you'd be carrying half of it.*

102

ULYSSES.
[Aside] 'A would have ten shares.

*He'd take the lot.*

AJAX.
I will knead him, I'll make him supple.

*I'll knead him like dough, I'll soften him up.*

NESTOR.
[Aside] He's not yet through warm. Force him with praises;
pour in, pour in; his ambition is dry.

*He's not yet cooked. Make him rise with praises;*
*pour them in to him; his ambition is dry.*

ULYSSES.
[To AGAMEMNON] My lord, you feed too much on this dislike.

*My lord, you're thinking too much about Achilles' behaviour.*

NESTOR.
Our noble general, do not do so.

*Our noble general, don't do so.*

DIOMEDES.
You must prepare to fight without Achilles.

*You must prepare to fight without Achilles.*

ULYSSES.
Why 'tis this naming of him does him harm.
Here is a man-but 'tis before his face;
I will be silent.

*It's thinking we can't do without him that causes the mischief.*
*There's a man here- but I can't speak about him*
*in front of his face.*

NESTOR.
Wherefore should you so?

He is not emulous, as Achilles is.

*Why should you?*
*He's not greedy for praise like Achilles.*

ULYSSES.
Know the whole world, he is as valiant.

*The whole world knows he's just as brave.*

AJAX.
A whoreson dog, that shall palter with us thus!
Would he were a Troyan!

*A son of a bitch, who thinks he can mess us about!*
*I wish he was a Trojan!*

NESTOR.
What a vice were it in Ajax now-

*What a vice it would be if Ajax now-*

ULYSSES.
If he were proud.

*If he was proud.*

DIOMEDES.
Or covetous of praise.

*Or desperate for praise.*

ULYSSES.
Ay, or surly borne.

*Yes, or with a bad attitude.*

DIOMEDES.
Or strange, or self-affected.

*Or haughty, or conceited.*

ULYSSES.
Thank the heavens, lord, thou art of sweet composure.

Praise him that gat thee, she that gave thee suck;
Fam'd be thy tutor, and thy parts of nature
Thrice-fam'd beyond, beyond all erudition;
But he that disciplin'd thine arms to fight-
Let Mars divide eternity in twain
And give him half; and, for thy vigour,
Bull-bearing Milo his addition yield
To sinewy Ajax. I will not praise thy wisdom,
Which, like a bourn, a pale, a shore, confines
Thy spacious and dilated parts. Here's Nestor,
Instructed by the antiquary times-
He must, he is, he cannot but be wise;
But pardon, father Nestor, were your days
As green as Ajax' and your brain so temper'd,
You should not have the eminence of him,
But be as Ajax.

*Thank goodness, lord, that you have a sweet nature.*
*I give thanks to your father and mother;*
*let your teacher be famous, and your natural talents*
*be three times more, beyond all intellect;*
*but the one who taught you how to fight-*
*let Mars split eternal fame in two*
*and give you half; as for your strength,*
*bull-carrying Milo will have to cede his title*
*to muscly Ajax. I will not praise your wisdom,*
*which is like a boundary, a fence, a shore, which*
*runs all round your great gifts. Here's Nestor,*
*who has learned from the ancients-*
*he must be, he is, he can't help but be wise;*
*but, if you'll pardon me, father Nestor, if you were as*
*young as Ajax, with the same mind you have,*
*you would not be greater than him,*
*you'd be equals.*

AJAX.
Shall I call you father?

*Shall I call you father?*

ULYSSES.
Ay, my good son.

*Yes, my good son.*

DIOMEDES.
Be rul'd by him, Lord Ajax.

*Follow his orders, lord Ajax.*

ULYSSES.
There is no tarrying here; the hart Achilles
Keeps thicket. Please it our great general
To call together all his state of war;
Fresh kings are come to Troy. To-morrow
We must with all our main of power stand fast;
And here's a lord-come knights from east to west
And cull their flower, Ajax shall cope the best.

*It's no use waiting here; Achilles won't*
*come out of hiding. If our great general agrees,*
*gather together all his forces;*
*Troy shall have new rulers. Tomorrow*
*we must put out our full strength;*
*and we have a lord - knights can come from all over,*
*wanting to show off their chivalry; Ajax will match the best.*

AGAMEMNON.
Go we to council. Let Achilles sleep.
Light boats sail swift, though greater hulks draw deep.
Exeunt

*Let's go to council. Let Achilles sleep.*
*Light boats can travel swiftly while great ones need deep water.*

# ACT III

## SCENE 1. Troy. PRIAM'S palace

Music sounds within. Enter PANDARUS and a SERVANT

PANDARUS.
Friend, you-pray you, a word. Do you not follow the young
Lord Paris?

*Friend - a word with you, please.Don't you follow young Lord Paris?*

SERVANT.
Ay, sir, when he goes before me.

*Yes sir, when he's in front of me.*

PANDARUS.
You depend upon him, I mean?

*I mean, you depend on him?*

SERVANT.
Sir, I do depend upon the lord.

*Sir, I depend on the Lord.*

PANDARUS.
You depend upon a notable gentleman; I must needs praise
him.

*You depend upon an important gentleman; I need to praise
him.*

SERVANT.
The lord be praised!

*Praise the Lord!*

PANDARUS.
You know me, do you not?

*You know who I am, don't you?*

SERVANT.
Faith, sir, superficially.

*Vaguely, sir.*

PANDARUS.
Friend, know me better: I am the Lord Pandarus.

*Friend, you should know me better: I am the Lord Pandarus.*

SERVANT.
I hope I shall know your honour better.

*I hope I shall know your honour better.*

PANDARUS.
I do desire it.

*That's what I want.*

SERVANT.
You are in the state of grace?

*You are in the state of grace?*

PANDARUS.
Grace! Not so, friend; honour and lordship are my titles.
What music is this?

*Grace! Not me, friend; I am called 'honour' and 'lordship'.*
*What's this music?*

SERVANT.
I do but partly know, sir; it is music in parts.

*I only know parts sir; it's made of parts.*

PANDARUS.
Know you the musicians?

*Do you know the musicians?*

SERVANT.
Wholly, sir.

*Completely, sir.*

PANDARUS.
Who play they to?

*Who are they playing to?*

SERVANT.
To the hearers, sir.

*To the people who are listening, sir.*

PANDARUS.
At whose pleasure, friend?

*Whose pleasure is it?*

SERVANT.
At mine, sir, and theirs that love music.

*Mine, sir, and anyone who loves music.*

PANDARUS.
Command, I mean, friend.

*I mean who commands it, friend.*

SERVANT.
Who shall I command, sir?

*Who shall I command, sir?*

PANDARUS.
Friend, we understand not one another: I am too courtly,
and thou art too cunning. At whose request do these men play?

*Friend, we don't understand each other: I'm too polite,
and you're too devious. Who asked these men to play?*

SERVANT.
That's to't, indeed, sir. Marry, sir, at the request of

Paris my lord, who is there in person; with him the mortal Venus, the heart-blood of beauty, love's invisible soul-

*Now we've got to the point, sir.Well, sir, at the request of my lord, Paris, who is there himself; with him is the living Venus, the very heart and soul of beauty -*

PANDARUS.
Who, my cousin, Cressida?

*Who, my cousin Cressida?*

SERVANT.
No, sir, Helen. Could not you find out that by her attributes?

*No sir, Helen.Couldn't you tell from the description?*

PANDARUS.
It should seem, fellow, that thou hast not seen the Lady Cressida. I come to speak with Paris from the Prince Troilus; I will make a complimental assault upon him, for my business seethes.

*It would appear, fellow, that you haven't seen Lady Cressida.I've come from Prince Troilus to speak with Paris; I will attack him with compliments, for my business is on the boil.*

SERVANT.
Sodden business! There's a stew'd phrase indeed!

*Boiling business?There's an overcooked phrase!*

Enter PARIS and HELEN, attended

PANDARUS.
Fair be to you, my lord, and to all this fair company!
Fair desires, in all fair measure, fairly guide them-especially
to you, fair queen! Fair thoughts be your fair pillow.

*Fair wishes to you, my lord, and all this fair company!
May fair desires, in fair measures, fairly guide them–especially
you, fair Queen! May you havefair dreams.*

HELEN.
Dear lord, you are full of fair words.

*Dear lord, you are full of fair words.*

PANDARUS.
You speak your fair pleasure, sweet queen. Fair prince,
here is good broken music.

*You speak your fair pleasure, sweet queen. Fair Prince,
this is good broken music.*

PARIS.
You have broke it, cousin; and by my life, you shall make it
whole again; you shall piece it out with a piece of your
performance.

*You're the one who broke it, cousin; and I swear, you shall make it
whole again; you shall repair it with a bit of your own
singing.*

HELEN.
He is full of harmony.

*He looks full of harmony.*

PANDARUS.
Truly, lady, no.

*Truly, Lady, I'm not.*

HELEN.
O, sir-

*Oh, Sir–*

PANDARUS.
Rude, in sooth; in good sooth, very rude.

*Rough, I swear; in all honesty, I'm very unpolished.*

PARIS.
Well said, my lord. Well, you say so in fits.

*I agree, my lord. Though you don't always say this.*

PANDARUS.
I have business to my lord, dear queen. My lord, will you
vouchsafe me a word?

*I have business with my lord, dear queen. My lord, will you
allow me to have a word?*

HELEN.
Nay, this shall not hedge us out. We'll hear you sing,
certainly-

*No, you won't fob us off that easily. We'll definitely hear you sing–*

PANDARUS.
Well sweet queen, you are pleasant with me. But, marry,
thus, my lord: my dear lord and most esteemed friend, your
brother Troilus-

*Well, sweet queen, you are kind to me. But, look here,
my lord: my dear lord and my great friend, your
brother Troilus–*

HELEN.
My Lord Pandarus, honey-sweet lord-

*My Lord Pandarus, honey–sweet lord–*

PANDARUS.
Go to, sweet queen, go to-commends himself most
affectionately to you-

*Just a minute, sweet queen, just a minute–gives you his affectionate
greetings–*

HELEN.
You shall not bob us out of our melody. If you do, our
melancholy upon your head!

*You shan't cheat us of our song. If you do, our
sadness will be upon your head!*

PANDARUS.

Sweet queen, sweet queen; that's a sweet queen, i' faith.

*Sweet queen, sweet queen; you are a sweet queen, I swear.*

HELEN.
And to make a sweet lady sad is a sour offence.

*And to make a sweet lady sad is a sour offence.*

PANDARUS.
Nay, that shall not serve your turn; that shall it not,
in truth, la. Nay, I care not for such words; no, no. -And, my
lord, he desires you that, if the King call for him at supper,
you will make his excuse.

*No, that's not going to work; I should say not, definitely!*
*No, such talk can't affect me; no, no.–And, my*
*lord, he asks you that if the king asks where he is at supper,*
*you make an excuse for him.*

HELEN.
My Lord Pandarus!

*My Lord Pandarus!*

PANDARUS.
What says my sweet queen, my very very sweet queen?

*What's my sweet queen saying, my very very sweet queen?*

PARIS.
What exploit's in hand? Where sups he to-night?

*What is he playing at? Where is he eating tonight?*

HELEN.
Nay, but, my lord-

*No, but, my lord–*

PANDARUS.
What says my sweet queen?-My cousin will fall out with
you.

*What's my sweet queen saying?–Paris will be angry with you for interrupting.*

HELEN.
You must not know where he sups.

*He doesn't want you to know where he's eating.*

PARIS.
I'll lay my life, with my disposer Cressida.

*I'll bet my life he's eating with his mistress Cressida.*

PANDARUS.
No, no, no such matter; you are wide. Come, your disposer
is sick.

*No, no, nothing of the sort; you're wide of the mark. How could he,
Cressida is ill.*

PARIS.
Well, I'll make's excuse.

*Well, I'll make his excuses.*

PANDARUS.
Ay, good my lord. Why should you say Cressida?
No, your poor disposer's sick.

*Yes, my good lord. Why did you mention Cressida?
No, the poor girl is sick.*

PARIS.
I spy.

*I spy.*

PANDARUS.
You spy! What do you spy?-Come, give me an instrument.
Now, sweet queen.

*You spy! What do you spy? Come, give me an instrument.
Now, sweet queen.*

HELEN.

Why, this is kindly done.

*Well, thank you for agreeing.*

PANDARUS.
My niece is horribly in love with a thing you have, sweet
queen.

*My niece is desperately in love with something you have, sweet
queen.*

HELEN.
She shall have it, my lord, if it be not my Lord Paris.

*She shall have it, my lord, as long as it's not my Lord Paris.*

PANDARUS.
He! No, she'll none of him; they two are twain.

*Him! No, she doesn't want him; they have nothing in common.*

HELEN.
Falling in, after falling out, may make them three.

*Maybe after falling out they would make up, and then there might be three of them.*

PANDARUS.
Come, come. I'll hear no more of this; I'll sing you a
song now.

*Come along. No more of this talk; I'll sing you a
song now.*

HELEN.
Ay, ay, prithee now. By my troth, sweet lord, thou hast a
fine forehead.

*Yes, yes, now please. I swear, sweet lord, you have a
fine forehead.*

PANDARUS.
Ay, you may, you may.

*Get along with you.*

HELEN.
Let thy song be love. 'This love will undo us all.' O Cupid,
Cupid, Cupid!

*Sing a song about love. 'This love will undo us all.' Oh Cupid,*
*Cupid, Cupid!*

PANDARUS.
Love! Ay, that it shall, i' faith.

*Love! Yes, it certainly shall, I swear.*

PARIS.
Ay, good now, love, love, nothing but love.

*Yes, please, love, love, nothing but love.*

PANDARUS.
In good troth, it begins so.
[Sings]
Love, love, nothing but love, still love, still more!
For, oh, love's bow
Shoots buck and doe;
The shaft confounds
Not that it wounds,
But tickles still the sore.
These lovers cry, O ho, they die!
Yet that which seems the wound to kill
Doth turn O ho! to ha! ha! he!
So dying love lives still.
O ho! a while, but ha! ha! ha!
O ho! groans out for ha! ha! ha!-hey ho!

*Love, love, nothing but love, still love, still more!*
*For, oh, Cupid's arrow*
*hits the male and female;*
*the shaft overwhelms,*
*though it doesn't wound*
*it still tickles the gash.*

*And the lovers cry, 'Oh! Oh!', they die!*
*But what seems to be a fatal wound*
*then turns ' Oh! Oh!' To 'Ha, ha, he!'*

*So the love that was dying still lives.*
*'Oh! Oh!' for a while, but then 'Ha, ha, ha!'*
*'Oh ho!' groans into 'Ha! Ha! Ha! Hey-ho!'*

HELEN.
In love, i' faith, to the very tip of the nose.

*I swear he's got love off to a T.*

PARIS.
He eats nothing but doves, love; and that breeds hot blood,
and hot blood begets hot thoughts, and hot thoughts beget hot
deeds, and hot deeds is love.

*He eats nothing but doves, love; and that gives him hot blood,*
*and hot blood gives him hot thoughts, and hot thoughts start hot*
*deeds, and hot deeds make love.*

PANDARUS.
Is this the generation of love: hot blood, hot thoughts,
and hot deeds? Why, they are vipers. Is love a generation of
vipers? Sweet lord, who's a-field today?

*Is this how love is made: hot blood, hot thoughts,*
*and hot deeds? Why, they are terrible things. Is love made of*
*terrible things? Sweet lord, who's gone to the battle today?*

PARIS.
Hector, Deiphobus, Helenus, Antenor, and all the gallantry
of Troy. I would fain have arm'd to-day, but my Nell would not
have it so. How chance my brother Troilus went not?

*Hector, Deiphobus, Helenus, Antenor, and all the gallant men*
*of Troy. I would have gone today myself, but Helen would not*
*let me. Why didn't my brother Troilus go?*

HELEN.
He hangs the lip at something. You know all, Lord Pandarus.

*He's sticking his lip out at something. You know everything, Lord Pandarus.*

PANDARUS.
Not I, honey-sweet queen. I long to hear how they spend
to-day. You'll remember your brother's excuse?

*I don't, honey sweet queen. I can't wait to hear how they spent*
*the day. You'll remember to give your brother's excuses?*

PARIS.
To a hair.

*Just as you said.*

PANDARUS.
Farewell, sweet queen.

*Farewell, sweet queen.*

HELEN.
Commend me to your niece.

*Give my best to your niece.*

PANDARUS.
I will, sweet queen.

*I will, sweet queen.*

Exit. Sound a retreat

PARIS.
They're come from the field. Let us to Priam's hall
To greet the warriors. Sweet Helen, I must woo you
To help unarm our Hector. His stubborn buckles,
With these your white enchanting fingers touch'd,
Shall more obey than to the edge of steel
Or force of Greekish sinews; you shall do more
Than all the island kings-disarm great Hector.

*They've come from the field. Let's go to Priam's hall*
*to greet the warriors. Sweet Helen, I must ask you*
*if you would help take our Hector's armour off. His stubborn buckles,*
*touched with your enchanting white fingers,*
*will come off more easily than when attacked with swords*
*or Greek strength; you will do more*
*than all the kings of Greece can do- disarm great Hector.*

HELEN.

'Twill make us proud to be his servant, Paris;
Yea, what he shall receive of us in duty
Gives us more palm in beauty than we have,
Yea, overshines ourself.

*I will be proud to be his servant, Paris;*
*the duty I shall do him*
*will give me more credit than I have for my beauty,*
*it will make me greater.*

PARIS.
Sweet, above thought I love thee.

*Dearest, I love you more than you can imagine.*

Exeunt

# SCENE 2. Troy. PANDARUS' orchard

Enter PANDARUS and TROILUS' BOY, meeting

PANDARUS.
How now! Where's thy master? At my cousin Cressida's?

*Hello there! Where's your master? At my cousin Cressida's?*

BOY.
No, sir; he stays for you to conduct him thither.

*No, sir; he's waiting for you to take him there.*

Enter TROILUS

PANDARUS.
O, here he comes. How now, how now!

*Oh, here he comes. Hello there, hello!*

TROILUS.
Sirrah, walk off.

*Sir, off you go.*

Exit Boy

PANDARUS.
Have you seen my cousin?

*Have you seen my cousin?*

TROILUS.
No, Pandarus. I stalk about her door
Like a strange soul upon the Stygian banks
Staying for waftage. O, be thou my Charon,
And give me swift transportation to these fields
Where I may wallow in the lily beds
Propos'd for the deserver! O gentle Pandar,

From Cupid's shoulder pluck his painted wings,
And fly with me to Cressid!

*No, Pandarus. I hang around her door*
*like a soul on the banks of the Styx*
*waiting to be carried over. You be my ferryman,*
*and grant me swift passage to the Elysian Fields*
*where I can wallow in the beds of lilies*
*which are promised to the deserving! Oh gentle Pandarus,*
*steal the painted wings from Cupid's shoulder,*
*and fly with me to Cressida!*

PANDARUS.
Walk here i' th' orchard, I'll bring her straight.

*Walk here in the orchard, I'll bring her at once.*

Exit

TROILUS.
I am giddy; expectation whirls me round.
Th' imaginary relish is so sweet
That it enchants my sense; what will it be
When that the wat'ry palate tastes indeed
Love's thrice-repured nectar? Death, I fear me;
Swooning destruction; or some joy too fine,
Too subtle-potent, tun'd too sharp in sweetness,
For the capacity of my ruder powers.
I fear it much; and I do fear besides
That I shall lose distinction in my joys;
As doth a battle, when they charge on heaps
The enemy flying.

*I am dizzy; hope is spinning around.*
*Just imagining what could happen is so sweet*
*that it enchants my senses; what will it be like*
*when our starved palates actually get a real taste*
*of the pure nectar of love? I fear death,*
*or fainting fits, from some joy too wonderful,*
*too subtle and powerful, too overwhelmingly sweet*
*for my rough soul to cope with.*
*I'm very afraid of that; and I also fear*
*that I shall lose the ability to tell one joy from another,*
*like in a battle, when they charge indiscriminately*

*on the fleeing enemy.*

Re-enter PANDARUS

PANDARUS.
She's making her ready, she'll come straight; you must be
witty now. She does so blush, and fetches her wind so short, as
if she were fray'd with a sprite. I'll fetch her. It is the
prettiest villain; she fetches her breath as short as a new-ta'en
sparrow.

*She's getting herself ready, she'll come at once; you must be
sparkling now. She blushes so much, and breathes so heavily, as
if she had seen a ghost. I'll get her. She is the
most charming wretch; she's panting like a newly captured
sparrow.*

Exit

TROILUS.
Even such a passion doth embrace my bosom.
My heart beats thicker than a feverous pulse,
And all my powers do their bestowing lose,
Like vassalage at unawares encount'ring
The eye of majesty.

*The same excitement fills my soul.
My heart is beating faster than a sick man's pulse,
and all my faculties have lost their powers,
like a humble subject who has unexpectedly
found the King is looking at him.*

Re-enter PANDARUS With CRESSIDA

PANDARUS.
Come, come, what need you blush? Shame's a baby.-Here she
is now; swear the oaths now to her that you have sworn to me.-
What, are you gone again? You must be watch'd ere you be made
tame, must you? Come your ways, come your ways; an you draw
backward, we'll put you i' th' thills.-Why do you not speak to
her?-Come, draw this curtain and let's see your picture.
Alas the day, how loath you are to offend daylight! An 'twere
dark, you'd close sooner. So, so; rub on, and kiss the mistress.
How now, a kiss in fee-farm! Build there, carpenter; the air is

sweet. Nay, you shall fight your hearts out ere I part you. The
falcon as the tercel, for all the ducks i' th' river. Go to, go
to.

*Come now, why are you blushing? You're not a baby.—Here he
is now; now swear the oaths to her that you have sworn to me.—
What, have you gone again? I have to keep my eye on you before you
become tame, is that it? Come on, come on; if you go
backwards, we'll put a harness on you.—Why don't you speak to
her?—Let's take this veil away and see your face.
How unhappy for the day, that you don't want to show your face in the light! If
it was dark you'd get to grips sooner. That's it, on you go, and kiss the mistress.
What's this, a kiss which claims the property! Build there, carpenter ; the air is
sweet. Well, you would tear your hearts out before I parted you. The female
is just as keen as the male, I'll bet anything. Go on, go on.*

TROILUS.
You have bereft me of all words, lady.

*You have stripped me of all words, lady.*

PANDARUS.
Words pay no debts, give her deeds; but she'll bereave
you o' th' deeds too, if she call your activity in question.
What, billing again? Here's 'In witness whereof the parties
interchangeably.' Come in, come in; I'll go get a fire.

*Words won't pay the rent, give her deeds; but she'll strip you
of the deeds too, if she questions your manliness.
What, kissing again? Two parts of a single whole, clearly.
Come in, come in. I'll go and light the fire.*

Exit

CRESSIDA.
Will you walk in, my lord?

*Will you come in, my lord?*

TROILUS.
O Cressid, how often have I wish'd me thus!

*Oh Cressida, how often I've wished for this!*

CRESSIDA.
Wish'd, my lord! The gods grant-O my lord!

*Wished, my lord! The gods grant–oh my lord!*

TROILUS.
What should they grant? What makes this pretty abruption?
What too curious dreg espies my sweet lady in the fountain of our
love?

*What should they grant? What causes this sweet interruption?*
*What hidden dirt does my sweet lady see in the fountain of our*
*love?*

CRESSIDA.
More dregs than water, if my fears have eyes.

*More dirt than water, if my fears see correctly.*

TROILUS.
Fears make devils of cherubims; they never see truly.

*Fears make devils out of angels; they never see properly.*

CRESSIDA.
Blind fear, that seeing reason leads, finds safer footing
than blind reason stumbling without fear. To fear the worst oft
cures the worse.

*Blind fear, led by seeing reason, is on safer ground*
*than blind reason stumbling without fear. If you fear the worst,*
*you can often avoid it.*

TROILUS.
O, let my lady apprehend no fear! In all Cupid's pageant
there is presented no monster.

*Oh, don't let my lady be afraid! There's no such monster*
*in Cupid's plays.*

CRESSIDA.
Nor nothing monstrous neither?

*And nothing monstrous either?*

TROILUS.
Nothing, but our undertakings when we vow to weep seas,
live in fire, eat rocks, tame tigers; thinking it harder for our
mistress to devise imposition enough than for us to undergo any
difficulty imposed. This is the monstruosity in love, lady, that
the will is infinite, and the execution confin'd; that the desire
is boundless, and the act a slave to limit.

*Nothing, except our promises when we vow to weep seas,*
*live in fire, eat rocks, tame tigers; we think it's harder for our*
*mistress to invent difficult enough tasks for us rather than for us*
*to face any difficulty. This is the terrible thing in love, lady, that*
*desire is infinite, but exercising it has limitations; desire knows*
*no boundaries, but physically there are limits.*

CRESSIDA.
They say all lovers swear more performance than they are
able, and yet reserve an ability that they never perform; vowing
more than the perfection of ten, and discharging less than the
tenth part of one. They that have the voice of lions and the act
of hares, are they not monsters?

*They say all lovers promise to do more than they are*
*able, and yet they always hold something back; they promise*
*to be more perfect than ten men, but in practice they can't match*
*a tenth of one. People who roar like lions and act like hares,*
*aren't they monsters?*

TROILUS.
Are there such? Such are not we. Praise us as we are
tasted, allow us as we prove; our head shall go bare till merit
crown it. No perfection in reversion shall have a praise in
present. We will not name desert before his birth; and, being
born, his addition shall be humble. Few words to fair faith:
Troilus shall be such to Cressid as what envy can say worst shall
be a mock for his truth; and what truth can speak truest not
truer than Troilus.

*Are the people like that? I'm not. Give me my due praise according*
*to what you find; my head will be bare until you say it deserves*
*the crown. I don't ask for praise now for things I will do*
*in the future. I won't christen the baby before it's born, and when it is,*
*I shall be modest, I won't tempt fate. A few words to show the truth:*

*Troilus shall treat Cressida in such a way that the worst that the
envious could do would be to mock him for his fidelity; and the truest
speech of Truth himself will not be greater than the truth of Troilus.*

CRESSIDA.
Will you walk in, my lord?

*Will you come in, my lord?*

Re-enter PANDARUS

PANDARUS.
What, blushing still? Have you not done talking yet?

*What, blushing still? Haven't you done talking yet?*

CRESSIDA.
Well, uncle, what folly I commit, I dedicate to you.

*Well, uncle, whatever foolishness I get up to, I'll put it down to you.*

PANDARUS.
I thank you for that; if my lord get a boy of you, you'll
give him me. Be true to my lord; if he flinch, chide me for it.

*Thank you for that; if my lord gets you pregnant with a boy,
you'll give him to me. Be true to my lord; if he wavers, blame me for it.*

TROILUS.
You know now your hostages: your uncle's word and my firm
faith.

*Now you know your guarantees: you have your uncle's word and my
unwavering loyalty.*

PANDARUS.
Nay, I'll give my word for her too: our kindred, though
they be long ere they are wooed, they are constant being won;
they are burs, I can tell you; they'll stick where they are
thrown.

*No, I'll guarantee her too: our family, though
they take a long time to be wooed, they are faithful once they are won;
they are like burrs, I can tell you; they stick where they are thrown.*

CRESSIDA.
Boldness comes to me now and brings me heart.
Prince Troilus, I have lov'd you night and day
For many weary months.

*I feel bolder now and more courageous.*
*Prince Troilus, I have loved you night and day*
*for many long months.*

TROILUS.
Why was my Cressid then so hard to win?

*Then why was my Cressida so hard to win?*

CRESSIDA.
Hard to seem won; but I was won, my lord,
With the first glance that ever-pardon me.
If I confess much, you will play the tyrant.
I love you now; but till now not so much
But I might master it. In faith, I lie;
My thoughts were like unbridled children, grown
Too headstrong for their mother. See, we fools!
Why have I blabb'd? Who shall be true to us,
When we are so unsecret to ourselves?
But, though I lov'd you well, I woo'd you not;
And yet, good faith, I wish'd myself a man,
Or that we women had men's privilege
Of speaking first. Sweet, bid me hold my tongue,
For in this rapture I shall surely speak
The thing I shall repent. See, see, your silence,
Cunning in dumbness, from my weakness draws
My very soul of counsel. Stop my mouth.

*I made it hard to see that I was won, but I was won, my lord,*
*the first time you ever looked at–excuse me.*
*If I admit too much, you will lord it over me.*
*I love you now; but up until now not so much*
*that I couldn't control it. Actually, I'm lying;*
*my thoughts were like undisciplined children,*
*too much for their mother to control. Look, what fools we are!*
*Why have I spilled the beans? Who will keep our secrets,*
*when we can't keep them ourselves?*
*But, though I loved you greatly, I did not pursue you;*

*and yet, I swear, I wished that I was a man,*
*or that we women had the same right as men*
*to speak first. Dearest, tell me to hold my tongue,*
*for in my delirious joy I will surely say*
*something I shall regret. Look, look, your silence,*
*cunning in its dumbness, is using my weakness*
*to get my deepest thoughts out of me. Stop my mouth.*

TROILUS.
And shall, albeit sweet music issues thence.

*And I shall, although sweet music is coming from it.*

PANDARUS.
Pretty, i' faith.

*That's sweet, I must say.*

CRESSIDA.
My lord, I do beseech you, pardon me;
'Twas not my purpose thus to beg a kiss.
I am asham'd. O heavens! what have I done?
For this time will I take my leave, my lord.

*My Lord, I beg you to pardon me;*
*I didn't mean to beg a kiss like that.*
*I am ashamed. O heavens! What have I done?*
*I will leave you for now, my lord.*

TROILUS.
Your leave, sweet Cressid?

*You're leaving, sweet Cressida?*

PANDARUS.
Leave! An you take leave till to-morrow morning-

*Leave! There will be time enough for leaving tomorrow morning–*

CRESSIDA.
Pray you, content you.

*Enough of that, thank you.*

TROILUS.
What offends you, lady?

*What don't you like, lady?*

CRESSIDA.
Sir, mine own company.

*Sir, my own company.*

TROILUS.
You cannot shun yourself.

*You can't reject yourself.*

CRESSIDA.
Let me go and try.
I have a kind of self resides with you;
But an unkind self, that itself will leave
To be another's fool. I would be gone.
Where is my wit? I know not what I speak.

*Let me go and try.*
*Part of me wants to stay with you;*
*but another part of me rebels and says*
*it doesn't want to be another's fool. I will go.*
*Have I lost my mind? I don't know what to say.*

TROILUS.
Well know they what they speak that speak so wisely.

*Those who speak so wisely must know what they are saying.*

CRESSIDA.
Perchance, my lord, I show more craft than love;
And fell so roundly to a large confession
To angle for your thoughts; but you are wise-
Or else you love not; for to be wise and love
Exceeds man's might; that dwells with gods above.

*Perhaps, my lord, you think I show more cunning than love;*
*and gave such a free and open account of my feelings*
*to try and discover your thoughts; but you are wise–*
*or to put it another way you don't love me;no man can be*

*wise and in love at the same time; only the gods can do that.*

TROILUS.
O that I thought it could be in a woman-
As, if it can, I will presume in you-
To feed for aye her lamp and flames of love;
To keep her constancy in plight and youth,
Outliving beauty's outward, with a mind
That doth renew swifter than blood decays!
Or that persuasion could but thus convince me
That my integrity and truth to you
Might be affronted with the match and weight
Of such a winnowed purity in love.
How were I then uplifted! but, alas,
I am as true as truth's simplicity,
And simpler than the infancy of truth.

*Oh, I wish that it could be true that women–*
*and if it's true of any this will definitely be true of you–*
*could for ever keep her love light burning,*
*staying as loving as the first day she promised when young,*
*lasting longer than mere looks, with a mind*
*for love which grows faster than passion fades!*
*Or that something could convince me*
*that my faithfulness and loyalty to you*
*could be matched with the same amount*
*of such refined and pure love.*
*How wonderful that would be! But, alas,*
*I am as true as simple truth itself,*
*more innocent than Adam before the fall.*

CRESSIDA.
In that I'll war with you.

*I'll argue that point with you.*

TROILUS.
O virtuous fight,
When right with right wars who shall be most right!
True swains in love shall in the world to come
Approve their truth by Troilus, when their rhymes,
Full of protest, of oath, and big compare,
Want similes, truth tir'd with iteration-
As true as steel, as plantage to the moon,

As sun to day, as turtle to her mate,
As iron to adamant, as earth to th' centre-
Yet, after all comparisons of truth,
As truth's authentic author to be cited,
'As true as Troilus' shall crown up the verse
And sanctify the numbers.

*This is a virtuous fight,*
*when two who are right battle to see who is most right!*
*In the future true lovers shall use Troilus*
*as their example of fidelity, when their poems,*
*full of declarations, of promises, and great comparisons,*
*need similes, tired of repeating the truth–*
*'as true as steel, as fertile as the moon,*
*like sun to day, like a turtle to her mate,*
*like iron to a magnet, like the Earth to its centre–'*
*but, after all these illustrative similes,*
*in order to be shown as writing the truth,*
*'as true as Troilus' shall end the verse*
*and make the whole thing true.*

CRESSIDA.
Prophet may you be!
If I be false, or swerve a hair from truth,
When time is old and hath forgot itself,
When waterdrops have worn the stones of Troy,
And blind oblivion swallow'd cities up,
And mighty states characterless are grated
To dusty nothing-yet let memory
From false to false, among false maids in love,
Upbraid my falsehood when th' have said 'As false
As air, as water, wind, or sandy earth,
As fox to lamb, or to heifer's calf,
Pard to the hind, or stepdame to her son'-
Yea, let them say, to stick the heart of falsehood,
'As false as Cressid.'

*May your prediction come true!*
*If I am false, or deviate an inch from the truth,*
*when all recorded time is over,*
*when the raindrops have worn down the stones of Troy,*
*and all the cities have been forgotten,*
*and great states are nameless, ground down*
*to dust–may the memory of my falsehood*

*still be fresh amongst false maids in love,*
*and reprimand my falsehood when they have said 'as false*
*as air, as water, wind, or sandy earth,*
*as the fox to the lamb, or to the heifer's calf,*
*the leopard to the deer, or the stepmother to her son' –*
*then let them say, to really prove that someone is false,*
*'As false as Cressida.'*

PANDARUS.
Go to, a bargain made; seal it, seal it; I'll be the
witness. Here I hold your hand; here my cousin's. If ever you
prove false one to another, since I have taken such pains to
bring you together, let all pitiful goers-between be call'd to
the world's end after my name-call them all Pandars; let all
constant men be Troiluses, all false women Cressids, and all
brokers between Pandars. Say 'Amen.'

*Come on then, that's a bargain; seal it, seal it; I'll be the*
*witness. Here I take your hand; here I take my cousin's. If you ever*
*prove false to each other, let all the pitiful go-betweens be called*
*Pandars until the end of time; let all true men be called Troilus,*
*all false women Cressida, and all the go-betweens Pandars.*
*Say 'Amen.'*

TROILUS.
Amen.

*Amen.*

CRESSIDA.
Amen.

*Amen.*

PANDARUS.
Amen. Whereupon I will show you a chamber
and a bed; which bed, because it shall not speak of your
pretty encounters, press it to death. Away!
And Cupid grant all tongue-tied maidens here,
Bed, chamber, pander, to provide this gear!

*Amen. And now I will show you a room*
*and a bed; because this bed will never speak of your*
*lovely meeting, torture it as much as you like. Off you go!*

*And may Cupid give all the shy virgins here*
*a bed, a room and a go-between to provide them!*

Exeunt

# SCENE 3. The Greek camp

Flourish. Enter AGAMEMNON, ULYSSES, DIOMEDES, NESTOR, AJAX,

MENELAUS, and CALCHAS

CALCHAS.
Now, Princes, for the service I have done,
Th' advantage of the time prompts me aloud
To call for recompense. Appear it to your mind
That, through the sight I bear in things to come,
I have abandon'd Troy, left my possession,
Incurr'd a traitor's name, expos'd myself
From certain and possess'd conveniences
To doubtful fortunes, sequest'ring from me all
That time, acquaintance, custom, and condition,
Made tame and most familiar to my nature;
And here, to do you service, am become
As new into the world, strange, unacquainted-
I do beseech you, as in way of taste,
To give me now a little benefit
Out of those many regist'red in promise,
Which you say live to come in my behalf.

*Now, Princes, for the services I have performed,*
*this seems to me the right time*
*to ask for reward. I ask you to remember*
*that, because of what I can see in the future,*
*I have abandoned Troy, left my property,*
*taken the name of traitor, and gone from*
*solid comforts which I owned*
*to a doubtful future, cutting myself off from all*
*the things that time, acquaintance, custom and rank*
*had made most comfortable and familiar to me;*
*and here, in order to serve you, I have become*
*like a newborn baby, foreign, friendless–*
*I beg you, as a foretaste,*
*to now give me a little something*
*from all the things you have promised,*
*which you say will come to me in the future.*

AGAMEMNON.
What wouldst thou of us, Troyan? Make demand.

*What do you want from us, Trojan? Ask.*

CALCHAS.
You have a Troyan prisoner call'd Antenor,
Yesterday took; Troy holds him very dear.
Oft have you-often have you thanks therefore-
Desir'd my Cressid in right great exchange,
Whom Troy hath still denied; but this Antenor,
I know, is such a wrest in their affairs
That their negotiations all must slack
Wanting his manage; and they will almost
Give us a prince of blood, a son of Priam,
In change of him. Let him be sent, great Princes,
And he shall buy my daughter; and her presence
Shall quite strike off all service I have done
In most accepted pain.

*You have a Trojan prisoner called Antenor,*
*captured yesterday; Troy values him very highly.*
*You have frequently–and so I have frequently thanked you–*
*asked to exchange some great prisoner for my Cressida,*
*but Troy has always refused; but this Antenor,*
*I know, is so important to their business*
*that all their plans will go astray*
*if he's not there to manage them; and they would almost*
*give us a blood Prince, a son of Priam,*
*in exchange for him. Send him to them, great Princes,*
*and that will get my daughter; and having her here*
*will pay in full for all the trouble I have taken*
*on your behalf.*

AGAMEMNON.
Let Diomedes bear him,
And bring us Cressid hither. Calchas shall have
What he requests of us. Good Diomed,
Furnish you fairly for this interchange;
Withal, bring word if Hector will to-morrow
Be answer'd in his challenge. Ajax is ready.

*Let Diomedes take him there,*

*and bring Cressida here to us. Calchas shall have*
*what he asks for. Good Diomedes,*
*get everything ready for this the exchange;*
*also, bring news of whether Hector will*
*accept an answer to his challenge tomorrow. Ajax is ready.*

DIOMEDES.
This shall I undertake; and 'tis a burden
Which I am proud to bear.

*I shall do this; and I'm proud*
*to carry out the task.*

Exeunt DIOMEDES and CALCHAS

ACHILLES and PATROCLUS stand in their tent

ULYSSES.
Achilles stands i' th' entrance of his tent.
Please it our general pass strangely by him,
As if he were forgot; and, Princes all,
Lay negligent and loose regard upon him.
I will come last. 'Tis like he'll question me
Why such unplausive eyes are bent, why turn'd on him?
If so, I have derision med'cinable
To use between your strangeness and his pride,
Which his own will shall have desire to drink.
It may do good. Pride hath no other glass
To show itself but pride; for supple knees
Feed arrogance and are the proud man's fees.

*Achilles is standing at the entrance of his tent.*
*I think our general should ignore him as he passes,*
*as if he had forgotten about him; and, all you princes,*
*show that you don't pay him any mind.*
*I'll bring up the rear. He'll probably ask me*
*why he is getting such disapproving looks.*
*If he does I'll be able to tell him*
*the reason for it,*
*and he'll be so keen to hear about himself that he will listen.*
*It may do good. If he sees his own pride*
*reflected in you it might make him think; bowing the knee to him*
*will only feed his arrogance, it's what proud men like.*

AGAMEMNON.
We'll execute your purpose, and put on
A form of strangeness as we pass along.
So do each lord; and either greet him not,
Or else disdainfully, which shall shake him more
Than if not look'd on. I will lead the way.

*We'll carry out your plan, and pretend*
*not to see him as we pass by.*
*All of you do this; either don't greet him,*
*or greet him scornfully, which will disturb him more*
*than being ignored. I will lead the way.*

ACHILLES.
What comes the general to speak with me?
You know my mind. I'll fight no more 'gainst Troy.

*Why has the general come to speak to me?*
*You know what I think. I won't fight against Troy any more.*

AGAMEMNON.
What says Achilles? Would he aught with us?

*What's Achilles saying? Does he want something?*

NESTOR.
Would you, my lord, aught with the general?

*Is there something you want, my lord, with the general?*

ACHILLES.
No.

*No.*

NESTOR.
Nothing, my lord.

*Nothing, my lord.*

AGAMEMNON.
The better.

*That's good then.*

Exeunt AGAMEMNON and NESTOR

ACHILLES.
Good day, good day.

*Good day, good day.*

MENELAUS.
How do you? How do you?

*How are you? How are you?*

Exit

ACHILLES.
What, does the cuckold scorn me?

*What, is that cuckold scorning me?*

AJAX.
How now, Patroclus?

*How are you, Patroclus?*

ACHILLES.
Good morrow, Ajax.

*Good day, Ajax.*

AJAX.
Ha?

*Hmm?*

ACHILLES.
Good morrow.

*Good day.*

AJAX.
Ay, and good next day too.

*Yes, I expect tomorrow will be a good day as well.*

Exit

ACHILLES.
What mean these fellows? Know they not Achilles?

*What are these fellows up to? Don't they recognise Achilles?*

PATROCLUS.
They pass by strangely. They were us'd to bend,
To send their smiles before them to Achilles,
To come as humbly as they us'd to creep
To holy altars.

*They pass by in a strange way. They used to bow,*
*to put on a smile as they approached Achilles,*
*to come as humbly as if they were approaching*
*a holy altar.*

ACHILLES.
What, am I poor of late?
'Tis certain, greatness, once fall'n out with fortune,
Must fall out with men too. What the declin'd is,
He shall as soon read in the eyes of others
As feel in his own fall; for men, like butterflies,
Show not their mealy wings but to the summer;
And not a man for being simply man
Hath any honour, but honour for those honours
That are without him, as place, riches, and favour,
Prizes of accident, as oft as merit;
Which when they fall, as being slippery standers,
The love that lean'd on them as slippery too,
Doth one pluck down another, and together
Die in the fall. But 'tis not so with me:
Fortune and I are friends; I do enjoy
At ample point all that I did possess
Save these men's looks; who do, methinks, find out
Something not worth in me such rich beholding
As they have often given. Here is Ulysses.
I'll interrupt his reading.
How now, Ulysses!

*What, have I become a poor man?*
*It's certain that when a great man is out of luck*

*his friends soon desert him. When a man has fallen*
*he will know it as much from looking in the eyes of others*
*as he will from his own feelings; for men are like butterflies,*
*they don't show their powdered wings except in summer;*
*and no man gets any honour just for being a man,*
*he only gets honour for those honours which are*
*visible, like rank, riches and favour,*
*which are got by luck as often as by merit;*
*when they fall, for they have weak foundations,*
*the love that depended on them proves just as weak,*
*they both fall together, and they both*
*die in the fall. But I'm not like that:*
*Fortune favours me; I still have all*
*the great things that I had before,*
*apart from these men's glances; I think they*
*think that there is something about me which makes me*
*not as worth acknowledging as previously. Here is Ulysses.*
*I'll interrupt his reading.*
*Hello there, Ulysses!*

ULYSSES.
Now, great Thetis' son!

*Well then, great son of Thetis!*

ACHILLES.
What are you reading?

*What are you reading?*

ULYSSES.
A strange fellow here
Writes me that man-how dearly ever parted,
How much in having, or without or in-
Cannot make boast to have that which he hath,
Nor feels not what he owes, but by reflection;
As when his virtues shining upon others
Heat them, and they retort that heat again
To the first giver.

*This strange fellow*
*writes that a man–however good his attributes,*
*however much he has, inside or out–*
*can only measure what he has,*

*or enjoy what he owns, in the reflection of others;*
*his virtue shines on others*
*and heats them, and they give that heat back again*
*to the one who first gave it.*

ACHILLES.
This is not strange, Ulysses.
The beauty that is borne here in the face
The bearer knows not, but commends itself
To others' eyes; nor doth the eye itself-
That most pure spirit of sense-behold itself,
Not going from itself; but eye to eye opposed
Salutes each other with each other's form;
For speculation turns not to itself
Till it hath travell'd, and is mirror'd there
Where it may see itself. This is not strange at all.

*That's not strange, Ulysses.*
*A man cannot know the beauty*
*of his own face, he sees it*
*through the eyes of others; nor can the eye itself–*
*the most perfect all the senses–see itself,*
*it can't turn in on itself; but eyes that look at each other*
*greet each other with their own beauty;*
*sight cannot see itself*
*until it has gone out and found a mirror*
*where it can be reflected. This is not strange at all.*

ULYSSES.
I do not strain at the position-
It is familiar-but at the author's drift;
Who, in his circumstance, expressly proves
That no man is the lord of anything,
Though in and of him there be much consisting,
Till he communicate his parts to others;
Nor doth he of himself know them for aught
Till he behold them formed in th' applause
Where th' are extended; who, like an arch, reverb'rate
The voice again; or, like a gate of steel
Fronting the sun, receives and renders back
His figure and his heat. I was much rapt in this;
And apprehended here immediately
Th' unknown Ajax. Heavens, what a man is there!
A very horse that has he knows not what!

Nature, what things there are
Most abject in regard and dear in use!
What things again most dear in the esteem
And poor in worth! Now shall we see to-morrow-
An act that very chance doth throw upon him-
Ajax renown'd. O heavens, what some men do,
While some men leave to do!
How some men creep in skittish Fortune's-hall,
Whiles others play the idiots in her eyes!
How one man eats into another's pride,
While pride is fasting in his wantonness!
To see these Grecian lords!-why, even already
They clap the lubber Ajax on the shoulder,
As if his foot were on brave Hector's breast,
And great Troy shrinking.

*I'm not arguing with the point–*
*it's well known–but with the author's conclusions,*
*because in his explanation he clearly argues*
*that no man is the lord of anything,*
*however good he is in and of himself,*
*until he has shown his good qualities to others;*
*nor can he himself value them*
*until he sees them applauded*
*when he uses them–it's like an arch*
*echoing with your voice, or like a steel gate*
*facing the sun, which receives and sends back*
*his light and heat. I was very taken with this,*
*and saw immediately that it applied*
*to the unknown Ajax. Heavens, what a man he is!*
*He's like a horse that doesn't know his own strength.*
*Nature, how many things there are*
*that are thought of as worthless but are valuable in practice!*
*And how many things are there that people value*
*which are actually worthless! Now tomorrow we shall see*
*something happening that chance has thrown his way.*
*Ajax famous? O heavens, look at what some men do,*
*while others don't do what they should!*
*Some men go to beg changeable fortune,*
*while others throw away what she has given!*
*Look how one man can steal another's glory,*
*while the proud man is starving himself of it through arrogance!*
*Look at these Greek lords! Why, even now*
*they clap the idiot lout Ajax on the shoulder,*

*as if he had already got brave Hector under his heel,*
*and all of great Troy was terrified.*

ACHILLES.
I do believe it; for they pass'd by me
As misers do by beggars-neither gave to me
Good word nor look. What, are my deeds forgot?

*I can believe it; for they passed me by*
*like misers walking past beggars–they didn't give me either*
*good words or kind looks. What, have my deeds been forgotten?*

ULYSSES.
Time hath, my lord, a wallet at his back,
Wherein he puts alms for oblivion,
A great-siz'd monster of ingratitudes.
Those scraps are good deeds past, which are devour'd
As fast as they are made, forgot as soon
As done. Perseverance, dear my lord,
Keeps honour bright. To have done is to hang
Quite out of fashion, like a rusty mail
In monumental mock'ry. Take the instant way;
For honour travels in a strait so narrow -
Where one but goes abreast. Keep then the path,
For emulation hath a thousand sons
That one by one pursue; if you give way,
Or hedge aside from the direct forthright,
Like to an ent'red tide they all rush by
And leave you hindmost;
Or, like a gallant horse fall'n in first rank,
Lie there for pavement to the abject rear,
O'er-run and trampled on. Then what they do in present,
Though less than yours in past, must o'ertop yours;
For Time is like a fashionable host,
That slightly shakes his parting guest by th' hand;
And with his arms out-stretch'd, as he would fly,
Grasps in the corner. The welcome ever smiles,
And farewell goes out sighing. O, let not virtue seek
Remuneration for the thing it was;
For beauty, wit,
High birth, vigour of bone, desert in service,
Love, friendship, charity, are subjects all
To envious and calumniating Time.
One touch of nature makes the whole world kin-

144

That all with one consent praise new-born gawds,
Though they are made and moulded of things past,
And give to dust that is a little gilt
More laud than gilt o'er-dusted.
The present eye praises the present object.
Then marvel not, thou great and complete man,
That all the Greeks begin to worship Ajax,
Since things in motion sooner catch the eye
Than what stirs not. The cry went once on thee,
And still it might, and yet it may again,
If thou wouldst not entomb thyself alive
And case thy reputation in thy tent,
Whose glorious deeds but in these fields of late
Made emulous missions 'mongst the gods themselves,
And drave great Mars to faction.

*Time, my lord, has a bag on his back,*
*in which he puts gifts for forgetfulness,*
*which is a huge ungrateful monster.*
*These scraps are the good deeds of the past, which are devoured*
*as quickly as they are made, forgotten as soon*
*as they are done. Perseverance, my dear lord,*
*is what keeps honour bright. To have done something makes you*
*most unfashionable, like a rusty suit of armour,*
*a forgotten trophy. Keep marching onwards;*
*glory goes along such a narrow path*
*that only one can walk it at a time. So stick to the path,*
*because jealous rivalry has a thousand sons,*
*following in single file; if you give way,*
*or step aside from the straight path,*
*they'll rush by you like a tide*
*and leave you in last place;*
*or, like a brave horse that fell in the front rank,*
*you'll lie there as a stepping stone for the cowardly followers,*
*overrun and trampled on. Then what they do in the present,*
*though it's less than what you did in the past, beats you;*
*for time is like a fashionable host*
*who gives his parting guest a quick handshake,*
*and hugs the newcomer with his arms outstretched as if*
*he was going to fly. He always smiles in welcome,*
*and sighs at those who leave. No, there's no point in virtue*
*wanting credit for the things it has done;*
*for beauty, wit, high birth, bodily strength, good service,*
*love, friendship, charity, they are all*

*gobbled up by jealous and slandering Time.*
*There is one human weakness that everybody has,*
*which is that everybody praises newly minted things,*
*even if they are made and moulded by past events,*
*and they give more praise to trivial things that glitter*
*than solid gold which has a little dust on it.*
*The most recent eye praises the most recent object.*
*So don't be surprised, you great and accomplished man,*
*that all the Greeks have begun to worship Ajax,*
*since things which are moving catch the eye better*
*than things which are still. They once gave you their praise,*
*and they might even now, yes, again,*
*if you wouldn't bury yourself alive*
*and imprison your reputation in your tent,*
*one whose glorious deeds on this battlefield just recently*
*made even the gods join in the war,*
*and even great Mars took a side.*

ACHILLES.
Of this my privacy
I have strong reasons.

*I have good reason*
*for my isolation.*

ULYSSES.
But 'gainst your privacy
The reasons are more potent and heroical.
'Tis known, Achilles, that you are in love
With one of Priam's daughters.

*But against your isolation*
*there are more powerful and heroic reasons.*
*It's known, Achilles, that you're in love*
*with one of Priam's daughters.*

ACHILLES.
Ha! known!

*Ha! known!*

ULYSSES.
Is that a wonder?
The providence that's in a watchful state

Knows almost every grain of Plutus' gold;
Finds bottom in th' uncomprehensive deeps;
Keeps place with thought, and almost, like the gods,
Do thoughts unveil in their dumb cradles.
There is a mystery-with whom relation
Durst never meddle-in the soul of state,
Which hath an operation more divine
Than breath or pen can give expressure to.
All the commerce that you have had with Troy
As perfectly is ours as yours, my lord;
And better would it fit Achilles much
To throw down Hector than Polyxena.
But it must grieve young Pyrrhus now at home,
When fame shall in our island sound her trump,
And all the Greekish girls shall tripping sing
'Great Hector's sister did Achilles win;
But our great Ajax bravely beat down him.'
Farewell, my lord. I as your lover speak.
The fool slides o'er the ice that you should break.

*Is it any surprise?*
*The prudent management of a watchful nation*
*knows every grain of gold it owns;*
*it reaches down to the bottom of the ocean;*
*it moves as rapidly as thought, and almost, like the gods,*
*knows your thoughts before they are spoken.*
*There is a mystery–which should not be*
*discussed–about the heart of a nation,*
*which works in a way which is more godlike*
*than speech or writing can express.*
*All the dealings you have had with Troy*
*are known to us as well as they are to yourself, my lord;*
*it would be more suitable for Achilles*
*to lay down Hector than Polyxena.*
*But your young son Pyrrhus who is now at home*
*will surely get upset when the rumours reach our islands*
*and all the Greek girls will dance and sing:*
*'Achilles won great Hector's sister,*
*but it was our great Ajax who bravely beat Hector.'*
*Farewell, my lord. I'm speaking as your friend;*
*the fool can get away with things that will ruin you.*

Exit

PATROCLUS.
To this effect, Achilles, have I mov'd you.
A woman impudent and mannish grown
Is not more loath'd than an effeminate man
In time of action. I stand condemn'd for this;
They think my little stomach to the war
And your great love to me restrains you thus.
Sweet, rouse yourself; and the weak wanton Cupid
Shall from your neck unloose his amorous fold,
And, like a dew-drop from the lion's mane,
Be shook to airy air.

*This is what I have been telling you, Achilles.*
*A woman who has become shameless and manlike*
*isn't more horrible than a womanish man*
*when it's time for action. I am criticised for this;*
*they think my dislike of the war*
*and your great love for me is holding you back.*
*Dearest, rouse yourself; and the weak lusty Cupid*
*shall release his amorous hold on your neck,*
*and be shaken off into the empty air*
*like a dew drop from a lion's mane.*

ACHILLES.
Shall Ajax fight with Hector?

*Will Ajax fight with Hector?*

PATROCLUS.
Ay, and perhaps receive much honour by him.

*Yes, and maybe get great glory from it.*

ACHILLES.
I see my reputation is at stake;
My fame is shrewdly gor'd.

*I see my reputation is at stake;*
*my fame is badly wounded.*

PATROCLUS.
O, then, beware:
Those wounds heal ill that men do give themselves;
Omission to do what is necessary

Seals a commission to a blank of danger;
And danger, like an ague, subtly taints
Even then when they sit idly in the sun.

*Well beware then;*
*self-inflicted wounds heal badly;*
*failing to do what is necessary*
*gives danger a blank cheque;*
*and danger, like a fever, creeps over us,*
*even when we are just sitting idly in the sun.*

ACHILLES.
Go call Thersites hither, sweet Patroclus.
I'll send the fool to Ajax, and desire him
T' invite the Troyan lords, after the combat,
To see us here unarm'd. I have a woman's longing,
An appetite that I am sick withal,
To see great Hector in his weeds of peace;
To talk with him, and to behold his visage,
Even to my full of view.

Enter THERSITES

A labour sav'd!

*Go and call Thersites here, sweet Patroclus.*
*I'll send the fool to Ajax, and ask him*
*to invite the Trojan Lords, after the combat,*
*to visit us here unarmed. I have a desperate longing,*
*like a woman, that's making me sick,*
*to see great Hector out of his armour;*
*to talk with him, and to see his face,*
*to get my fill of it.*

*There's a trouble saved.*

THERSITES.
A wonder!

*Amazing!*

ACHILLES.
What?

*What?*

THERSITES.
Ajax goes up and down the field asking for himself.

*Ajax is going up and down the field, calling for himself.*

ACHILLES.
How so?

*Want you mean?*

THERSITES.
He must fight singly to-morrow with Hector, and is so
prophetically proud of an heroical cudgelling that he raves in
saying nothing.

*He is having a single combat tomorrow with Hector, and is so
certain that he is going to give him an heroic beating
that he raves incoherently.*

ACHILLES.
How can that be?

*What is he doing?*

THERSITES.
Why, 'a stalks up and down like a peacock-a stride and a
stand; ruminaies like an hostess that hath no arithmetic but her
brain to set down her reckoning, bites his lip with a politic
regard, as who should say 'There were wit in this head, an
'twould out'; and so there is; but it lies as coldly in him as
fire in a flint, which will not show without knocking. The man's
undone for ever; for if Hector break not his neck i' th' combat,
he'll break't himself in vainglory. He knows not me. I said 'Good
morrow, Ajax'; and he replies 'Thanks, Agamemnon.' What think you
of this man that takes me for the general? He's grown a very land
fish, languageless, a monster. A plague of opinion! A man may
wear it on both sides, like leather jerkin.

*Well, he marches up and down like a peacock, strutting and
standing. He stands thinking like a landlady who has to add up
the bill in her head, bites his lip with a wise look,
as if one should say, 'there is intelligence in this head,*

and we shall see it'; and there is too, but in him it's as cold as
fire in flint, you can't get it out without bashing it. The man is
lost for ever; because if Hector doesn't break his neck in the fight,
he'll break himself with vanity. He didn't recognise me. I said 'good
day, Ajax'; and he replied 'thanks, Agamemnon.' What do you think
of this man who mistakes me for the general? He's a fish out of
water, a speechless monster. Damn this business of what men think of themselves!
A man can wear it whichever way he wants, like a jerkin.

ACHILLES.
Thou must be my ambassador to him, Thersites.

*You must be my ambassador to him, Thersites.*

THERSITES.
Who, I? Why, he'll answer nobody; he professes not
answering. Speaking is for beggars: he wears his tongue in's
arms. I will put on his presence. Let Patroclus make his demands
to me, you shall see the pageant of Ajax.

*Who, me? Why, he'll speak to nobody; he is determined he will not
answer. Speaking is for beggars, his way of speaking is with his
weapons. I'll show you what he looks like. Let Patroclus ask me
his questions, I'll give you a show of Ajax.*

ACHILLES.
To him, Patroclus. Tell him I humbly desire the valiant
Ajax to invite the most valourous Hector to come unarm'd to my
tent; and to procure safe conduct for his person of the
magnanimous and most illustrious six-or-seven-times-honour'd
Captain General of the Grecian army, et cetera, Agamemnon. Do
this.

*Speak to him, Patroclus. Tell him that I humbly request the brave
Ajax to invite the most courageous Hector to come unarmed to my
tent; and to get a guarantee of safe conduct for him from the
generous and most exalted many times honoured
Captain General of the Greek army, and so forth, Agamemnon. Do
this.*

PATROCLUS.
Jove bless great Ajax!

*Jove bless great Ajax!*

THERSITES.
Hum!

*Hum!*

PATROCLUS.
I come from the worthy Achilles-

*I have come from the good Achilles–*

THERSITES.
Ha!

*Ha!*

PATROCLUS.
Who most humbly desires you to invite Hector to his
tent-

*Who most humbly requests that you invite Hector to his
tent-*

THERSITES.
Hum!

*Hum!*

PATROCLUS.
And to procure safe conduct from Agamemnon.

*And that you obtain a safe conduct from Agamemnon.*

THERSITES.
Agamemnon!

*Agamemnon!*

PATROCLUS.
Ay, my lord.

*Yes, my lord.*

THERSITES.

Ha!

*Ha!*

PATROCLUS.
What you say to't?

*What's your answer?*

THERSITES.
God buy you, with all my heart.

*With all my heart, goodbye.*

PATROCLUS.
Your answer, sir.

*What is your answer, sir?*

THERSITES.
If to-morrow be a fair day, by eleven of the clock it
will go one way or other. Howsoever, he shall pay for me ere he
has me.

*If there is good weather tomorrow, by eleven o'clock it
will have been decided one way or the other. Whatever happens
he's going to have to suffer to beat me.*

PATROCLUS.
Your answer, sir.

*Give me your answer, sir.*

THERSITES.
Fare ye well, with all my heart.

*With all my heart, farewell.*

ACHILLES.
Why, but he is not in this tune, is he?

*He isn't really singing this tune, is he?*

THERSITES.

No, but he's out a tune thus. What music will be in him
when Hector has knock'd out his brains I know not; but, I am sure,
none; unless the fiddler Apollo get his sinews to make callings
on.

*No, but this is what he's singing out of tune. What music he'll have left*
*when Hector has knocked his brains out I don't know; but, I am certain,*
*there won't be any; unless Apollo takes his sinews and makes strings out of them.*

ACHILLES.
Come, thou shalt bear a letter to him straight.

*Come on, you shall take him a letter at once.*

THERSITES.
Let me carry another to his horse; for that's the more
capable creature.

*Give me another one to take to his horse; that's the one*
*with more brains.*

ACHILLES.
My mind is troubled, like a fountain stirr'd;
And I myself see not the bottom of it.
Exeunt ACHILLES and PATROCLUS

*My mind is troubled, like a stream that has been stirred up;*
*I can't see to the bottom of it.*

THERSITES.
Would the fountain of your mind were clear again, that I
might water an ass at it. I had rather be a tick in a sheep than
such a valiant ignorance.

*I wish the stream of your mind was running clear again, so I*
*could bring an ass to drink at it. I'd rather be a tick on a sheep than*
*have such brave stupidity.*

Exit

154

# ACT IV

# SCENE 1. Troy. A street

Enter, at one side, AENEAS, and serva, and servant with a torch; at another, PARIS, DEIPHOBUS, ANTENOR, DIOMEDES the Grecian, and others, with torches

PARIS.
See, ho! Who is that there?

*Hello! Who's that over there?*

DEIPHOBUS.
It is the Lord Aeneas.

*It is the Lord Aeneas.*

AENEAS.
Is the Prince there in person?
Had I so good occasion to lie long
As you, Prince Paris, nothing but heavenly business
Should rob my bed-mate of my company.

*Is that the Prince himself?*
*If I had such a good reason to stay in bed late*
*as you, Prince Paris, nothing but business with the gods*
*would get me away from my bed mate.*

DIOMEDES.
That's my mind too. Good morrow, Lord Aeneas.

*That's what I think. Good day, Lord Aeneas.*

PARIS.
A valiant Greek, Aeneas -take his hand:
Witness the process of your speech, wherein
You told how Diomed, a whole week by days,
Did haunt you in the field.

*A brave Greek, Aeneas–take his hand:*
*remember what you yourself said, when*
*you told us how Diomedes followed you around*

*the battlefield every day for a week.*

AENEAS.
Health to you, valiant sir,
During all question of the gentle truce;
But when I meet you arm'd, as black defiance
As heart can think or courage execute.

*I wish you good health, brave Sir,*
*during this time of peaceful truce;*
*but when I meet you on the battlefield, I offer the sternest defiance*
*the heart can imagine or courage enact.*

DIOMEDES.
The one and other Diomed embraces.
Our bloods are now in calm; and so long health!
But when contention and occasion meet,
By Jove, I'll play the hunter for thy life
With all my force, pursuit, and policy.

*Diomedes welcomes both.*
*Everything is peaceful now, and so good health to you!*
*But come the time we meet on the battlefield,*
*by Jove, I shall hunt you down*
*with all my strength, speed and cunning.*

AENEAS.
And thou shalt hunt a lion, that will fly
With his face backward. In humane gentleness,
Welcome to Troy! now, by Anchises' life,
Welcome indeed! By Venus' hand I swear
No man alive can love in such a sort
The thing he means to kill, more excellently.

*And you shall be hunting a lion, that will fly*
*facing backwards. In the name of polite brotherhood,*
*welcome to Troy! Now, on my father's life,*
*you are very welcome! I swear by the hand of Venus*
*there isn't a man alive who can love the thing*
*that he plans to kill as much as I do.*

DIOMEDES.
We sympathise. Jove let Aeneas live,
If to my sword his fate be not the glory,

A thousand complete courses of the sun!
But in mine emulous honour let him die
With every joint a wound, and that to-morrow!

*I feel the same. If Aeneas isn't destined to*
*glorify my sword by dying on it, then may Jove*
*let him live a thousand years!*
*But my rivalry for glory makes me wish that he would die*
*with a wound in every joint, and that it would happen tomorrow!*

AENEAS.
We know each other well.

*We understand each other well.*

DIOMEDES.
We do; and long to know each other worse.

*We do; and we long to understand each other badly.*

PARIS.
This is the most despiteful'st gentle greeting
The noblest hateful love, that e'er I heard of.
What business, lord, so early?

*This is the most contemptuous gentle greeting,*
*the noblest hateful love, that I ever heard of.*
*Why are you up so early, my lord?*

AENEAS.
I was sent for to the King; but why, I know not.

*The king sent for me, but I don't know why.*

PARIS.
His purpose meets you: 'twas to bring this Greek
To Calchas' house, and there to render him,
For the enfreed Antenor, the fair Cressid.
Let's have your company; or, if you please,
Haste there before us. I constantly believe-
Or rather call my thought a certain knowledge-
My brother Troilus lodges there to-night.
Rouse him and give him note of our approach,
With the whole quality wherefore; I fear

We shall be much unwelcome.

*The reason is in front of you: it was to bring this Greek*
*to Calchas' house, and there to hand over to him,*
*in exchange for Antenor, the lovely Cressida.*
*Come along with us, or, if you like,*
*hurry there before us. I certainly think—*
*or actually you can say I am absolutely certain—*
*that my brother Troilus is staying there tonight.*
*Wake him and tell him that we are coming,*
*and tell him all about why; I fear*
*we will be very unwelcome.*

AENEAS.
That I assure you:
Troilus had rather Troy were borne to Greece
Than Cressid borne from Troy.

*I can promise you that:*
*Troilus would rather have Troy given to Greece*
*than Cressida taken from Troy.*

PARIS.
There is no help;
The bitter disposition of the time
Will have it so. On, lord; we'll follow you.

*It can't be helped;*
*these terrible times*
*insist on it. Go on, lord; we'll follow you.*

AENEAS.
Good morrow, all.

*Good day, all.*

Exit with servant

PARIS.
And tell me, noble Diomed-faith, tell me true,
Even in the soul of sound good-fellowship-
Who in your thoughts deserves fair Helen best,
Myself or Menelaus?

*So tell me, noble Diomed, by heavens, tell me truly,*
*absolutely in the spirit of good friendship,*
*who, to your mind, deserves fair heaven most,*
*me or Menelaus?*

DIOMEDES.
Both alike:
He merits well to have her that doth seek her,
Not making any scruple of her soilure,
With such a hell of pain and world of charge;
And you as well to keep her that defend her,
Not palating the taste of her dishonour,
With such a costly loss of wealth and friends.
He like a puling cuckold would drink up
The lees and dregs of a flat tamed piece;
You, like a lecher, out of whorish loins
Are pleas'd to breed out your inheritors.
Both merits pois'd, each weighs nor less nor more;
But he as he, the heavier for a whore.

*Both the same.*
*The one who has looked for her, not caring about*
*the fact that she has slept with another, or that*
*there has been so much suffering and expense, deserves her;*
*and you deserve just as much to keep her as you defend her,*
*seeming not to notice her dishonour,*
*with such a costly loss of wealth and friends.*
*He, like a whining cuckold, wants to drink up the dregs,*
*get back to himself a used woman;*
*you, like a dirty fornicator, don't mind breeding*
*your children from a whore's belly.*
*You both deserve her equally, neither has a stronger case,*
*both the same. But who will feel guiltier about having a whore?*

PARIS.
You are too bitter to your country-woman.

*You are too bitter towards your countrywoman.*

DIOMEDES.
She's bitter to her country. Hear me, Paris:
For every false drop in her bawdy veins
A Grecian's life hath sunk; for every scruple
Of her contaminated carrion weight

A Troyan hath been slain; since she could speak,
She hath not given so many good words breath
As for her Greeks and Troyans suff'red death.

*She is bitter to her country. Listen to me, Paris:*
*for every drop of blood in her lusty veins*
*a Greek has lost his life; for every tiny part*
*of the weight of her rotting carcass*
*a Trojan has been killed; since she learned to speak*
*she has not spoken as many words as the number*
*of Greeks and Trojanswho have died for her.*

PARIS.
Fair Diomed, you do as chapmen do,
Dispraise the thing that you desire to buy;
But we in silence hold this virtue well:
We'll not commend what we intend to sell.
Here lies our way.

*Good Diomedes,, you're doing what merchants do,*
*running down the thing that you want to buy.*
*But we won't do the same thing;*
*we won't praise what we mean to get a high price for.*
*This is our way.*

Exeunt

# SCENE 2. Troy. The court of PANDARUS' house

Enter TROILUS and CRESSIDA

TROILUS.
Dear, trouble not yourself; the morn is cold.

*Dearest, don't let's get up. The morning is cold.*

CRESSIDA.
Then, sweet my lord, I'll call mine uncle down;
He shall unbolt the gates.

*Then, my sweet lord, I'll call my uncle down;
he shall unbolt the gates.*

TROILUS.
Trouble him not;
To bed, to bed! Sleep kill those pretty eyes,
And give as soft attachment to thy senses
As infants' empty of all thought!

*Don't bother him;
come back to bed! Close those pretty eyes in sleep,
and empty your mind of thought,
be like a child!*

CRESSIDA.
Good morrow, then.

*Good day to you, then.*

TROILUS.
I prithee now, to bed.

*Please, go to bed.*

CRESSIDA.
Are you aweary of me?

*Are you tired of me?*

TROILUS.
O Cressida! but that the busy day,
Wak'd by the lark, hath rous'd the ribald crows,
And dreaming night will hide our joys no longer,
I would not from thee.

*Oh Cressida! If it weren't for the fact that the day,*
*awoken by the lark, has aroused the raucous crows,*
*and that the dreaming night will no longer keep our pleasures secret,*
*I wouldn't leave you.*

CRESSIDA.
Night hath been too brief.

*The night has been too short.*

TROILUS.
Beshrew the witch! with venomous wights she stays
As tediously as hell, but flies the grasps of love
With wings more momentary-swift than thought.
You will catch cold, and curse me.

*Dam the witch! With those who are evil spirited she stays*
*eternally, but she flies away from love*
*with wings as swift as thought.*
*You will catch cold, and curse me.*

CRESSIDA.
Prithee tarry.
You men will never tarry.
O foolish Cressid! I might have still held off,
And then you would have tarried. Hark! there's one up.

*Please stay,*
*you men never stay.*
*O foolish Cressida! I might still have waited,*
*and then you would have stayed. Listen! Someone is up.*

PANDARUS.
[Within] What's all the doors open here?

*Why are all the doors open here?*

TROILUS.
It is your uncle.

*It is your uncle.*

Enter PANDARUS

CRESSIDA.
A pestilence on him! Now will he be mocking.
I shall have such a life!

*Damnation to him! Now he will mock me.*
*I shall have such a time of it!*

PANDARUS.
How now, how now! How go maidenheads?
Here, you maid! Where's my cousin Cressid?

*Hello there, hello there! What price for virginity?*
*Hey, you girl! Where's my cousin Cressida?*

CRESSIDA.
Go hang yourself, you naughty mocking uncle.
You bring me to do, and then you flout me too.

*Go and hang yourself, you naughty mocking uncle.*
*You encourage me to do this, and now you mock me for it.*

PANDARUS.
To do what? to do what? Let her say what.
What have I brought you to do?

*To do what? To do what? Let her tell me what.*
*What have I encouraged you to do?*

CRESSIDA.
Come, come, beshrew your heart! You'll ne'er be good,
Nor suffer others.

*Enough of this, curses on your heart! You've got such a dirty mind,*
*you can't believe anyone else is different.*

PANDARUS.

164

Ha, ha! Alas, poor wretch! a poor capocchia! hast not
slept to-night? Would he not, a naughty man, let it sleep? A
bugbear take him!

*Ha, ha! Alas, poor wretch! Poor simpleton! Haven't you
slept tonight? Wouldn't that naughty man let you sleep? May
a goblin take him away!*

CRESSIDA.
Did not I tell you? Would he were knock'd i' th' head!
[One knocks]
Who's that at door? Good uncle, go and see.
My lord, come you again into my chamber.
You smile and mock me, as if I meant naughtily.

*What did I say? I wish someone would bash him on the head!
[Somebody knocks]
Who's that at the door? Good uncle, go and see.
My lord, you come back into my bedroom.
You smile and laugh at me, as if I had naughty intentions.*

TROILUS.
Ha! ha!

*Ha! Ha!*

CRESSIDA.
Come, you are deceiv'd, I think of no such thing.
[Knock]
How earnestly they knock! Pray you come in:
I would not for half Troy have you seen here.

*Come, you are mistaken, I'm thinking of no such thing.
[Knock]
How persistently they knock! Please come in:
I wouldn't want have you seen here for half of Troy.*

Exeunt TROILUS and CRESSIDA

PANDARUS.
Who's there? What's the matter? Will you beat down the
door? How now? What's the matter?

*Who's there? What's the matter? Do you want to knock down the door? What's going on? What's the matter?*

Enter AENEAS

AENEAS.
Good morrow, lord, good morrow.

*Good day to you, lord, good day.*

PANDARUS.
Who's there? My lord Aeneas? By my troth,
I knew you not. What news with you so early?

*Who's that? My lord Aeneas? I swear,
I didn't know it was you. What brings you here so early?*

AENEAS.
Is not Prince Troilus here?

*Isn't Prince Troilus here?*

PANDARUS.
Here! What should he do here?

*Here! What would he be doing here?*

AENEAS.
Come, he is here, my lord; do not deny him.
It doth import him much to speak with me.

*Come, he is here, my lord; don't deny it.
It's very important that he should speak with me.*

PANDARUS.
Is he here, say you? It's more than I know, I'll be
sworn. For my own part, I came in late. What should he do here?

*He's here, you say? That's more than I know, I'll
swear. As for me, I came in late. What would he be doing here?*

AENEAS.
Who!-nay, then. Come, come, you'll do him wrong ere you are
ware; you'll be so true to him to be false to him. Do not you
know of him, but yet go fetch him hither; go.

*What!–No, then. Come, come, you'll do him harm without*
*knowing it; your loyalty will actually make you disloyal. You can say you*
*don't know he's here, but still, go and get him; go.*

Re-enter TROILUS

TROILUS.
How now! What's the matter?

*What's this! What's the matter?*

AENEAS.
My lord, I scarce have leisure to salute you,
My matter is so rash. There is at hand
Paris your brother, and Deiphobus,
The Grecian Diomed, and our Antenor
Deliver'd to us; and for him forthwith,
Ere the first sacrifice, within this hour,
We must give up to Diomedes' hand
The Lady Cressida.

*My Lord, I hardly have time to greet you,*
*my business is so urgent. Nearby there is*
*Paris your brother, and Deiphobus,*
*the Greek Diomedes, and our Antenor*
*returned to us; and in return for him at once,*
*before the first sacrifice has been made, within the hour,*
*we must hand over the lady Cressida*
*to Diomedes.*

TROILUS.
Is it so concluded?

*This is what's been decided?*

AENEAS.
By Priam, and the general state of Troy.
They are at hand and ready to effect it.

*By Priam, and the general assembly of Troy.*
*They are almost here and ready to carry out the order.*

TROILUS.

How my achievements mock me!
I will go meet them; and, my lord Aeneas,
We met by chance; you did not find me here.

*How the fates mock what I have done!*
*I will go and meet them; and, my lord Aeneas,*
*we met by chance; you did not find me here.*

AENEAS.
Good, good, my lord, the secrets of nature
Have not more gift in taciturnity.

*Very well, my good lord, nature won't reveal her mysteries*
*any slower than I will give up your secret.*

Exeunt TROILUS and AENEAS

PANDARUS.
Is't possible? No sooner got but lost? The devil take
Antenor! The young prince will go mad. A plague upon Antenor! I
would they had broke's neck.

*Is this possible? No sooner does he get than lose her? Damnation to*
*Antenor! The young prince will go mad. A plague upon Antenor! I*
*wish they had broken his neck.*

Re-enter CRESSIDA

CRESSIDA.
How now! What's the matter? Who was here?

*Hello there! What's the matter? Who was here?*

PANDARUS.
Ah, ah!

*Ah, ah!*

CRESSIDA.
Why sigh you so profoundly? Where's my lord? Gone? Tell
me, sweet uncle, what's the matter?

*Why do you sigh so deeply? Where is my lord? Gone? Tell*
*me, sweet uncle, what's the matter?*

PANDARUS.
Would I were as deep under the earth as I am above!

*I wish I was as deep under the earth as I am above it!*

CRESSIDA.
O the gods! What's the matter?

*By the gods! What's the matter?*

PANDARUS.
Pray thee, get thee in. Would thou hadst ne'er been born!
I knew thou wouldst be his death! O, poor gentleman! A plague
upon Antenor!

*Please, get inside. I wish you had never been born!*
*I knew you would be the death of him! Oh, poor gentleman! A plague*
*on Antenor!*

CRESSIDA.
Good uncle, I beseech you, on my knees I beseech you,
what's the matter?

*Good uncle, I beg you, on my knees I beg you,*
*what's the matter?*

PANDARUS.
Thou must be gone, wench, thou must be gone; thou art
chang'd for Antenor; thou must to thy father, and be gone from
Troilus. 'Twill be his death; 'twill be his bane; he cannot bear
it.

*You must go, wench, you must go; you are to be*
*exchanged for Antenor; you must go to your father, and leave*
*Troilus. It will be the death of him; it will ruin him; he won't be able to*
*bear it.*

CRESSIDA.
O you immortal gods! I will not go.

*Oh you immortal gods! I will not go.*

PANDARUS.

Thou must.

*You must.*

CRESSIDA.
I will not, uncle. I have forgot my father;
I know no touch of consanguinity,
No kin, no love, no blood, no soul so near me
As the sweet Troilus. O you gods divine,
Make Cressid's name the very crown of falsehood,
If ever she leave Troilus! Time, force, and death,
Do to this body what extremes you can,
But the strong base and building of my love
Is as the very centre of the earth,
Drawing all things to it. I'll go in and weep-

*I will not, uncle. I have forgotten my father;*
*I feel no sense of blood relations,*
*no kinship, no love, no blood, no soul, is so dear to me*
*as the sweet Troilus. Oh you divine gods,*
*make Cressida's name proverbial for falsehood,*
*if she ever leaves Troilus! Time, compulsion, and death,*
*do whatever you can to this body,*
*but the strong foundation and building of my love*
*is like the very centre of the earth,*
*drawing all things to it. I'll go in and weep-*

PANDARUS.
Do, do.

*Yes, do that.*

CRESSIDA.
Tear my bright hair, and scratch my praised cheeks,
Crack my clear voice with sobs and break my heart,
With sounding 'Troilus.' I will not go from Troy.

*Tear my shining hair, and scratch my admired cheeks,*
*crack my sweet voice with sobs and break my heart,*
*saying 'Troilus.' I will not leave Troy.*

Exeunt

170

# SCENE 3. Troy. A street before PANDARUS' house

Enter PARIS, TROILUS, AENEAS, DEIPHOBUS, ANTENOR, and DIOMEDES

PARIS.
It is great morning; and the hour prefix'd
For her delivery to this valiant Greek
Comes fast upon. Good my brother Troilus,
Tell you the lady what she is to do
And haste her to the purpose.

*It's well on into the morning; and the time set
to hand her over to this brave Greek
is almost here. My good brother Troilus,
tell the lady what she is to do
and tell her to hurry.*

TROILUS.
Walk into her house.
I'll bring her to the Grecian presently;
And to his hand when I deliver her,
Think it an altar, and thy brother Troilus
A priest, there off'ring to it his own heart.

*Go in to her house.
I'll bring her to the Greek shortly;
and when I give her over to his hand,
think of it as an altar, with your brother Troilus
as a priest, sacrificing his own heart.*

Exit

PARIS.
I know what 'tis to love,
And would, as I shall pity, I could help!
Please you walk in, my lords.

*I know what it's like to love,
and I wish I could give as much help as I will pity!
Please go in, my lords.*

*Exeunt*

# SCENE 4. Troy. PANDARUS' house

Enter PANDARUS and CRESSIDA

PANDARUS.
Be moderate, be moderate.

*Calm down, calm down.*

CRESSIDA.
Why tell you me of moderation?
The grief is fine, full, perfect, that I taste,
And violenteth in a sense as strong
As that which causeth it. How can I moderate it?
If I could temporize with my affections
Or brew it to a weak and colder palate,
The like allayment could I give my grief.
My love admits no qualifying dross;
No more my grief, in such a precious loss.

*Why are you telling me to calm down?*
*This grief is fine, great, perfect, I can taste it,*
*and it's as terrible and violent*
*as the thing which is causing it. How can I calm it?*
*If I could negotiate with my passion,*
*or dilute it to suit someone with a weaker and colder appetite,*
*then I could do the same with my grief.*
*My love is absolutely pure;*
*so my grief is the same, when I suffer such a terrible loss.*

Enter TROILUS

PANDARUS.
Here, here, here he comes. Ah, sweet ducks!

*Here, here, here he comes. Ah, sweet ducks!*

CRESSIDA.
O Troilus! Troilus! [Embracing him]

*Oh Troilus! Troilus!*

PANDARUS.
What a pair of spectacles is here! Let me embrace too. 'O
heart,' as the goodly saying is,
O heart, heavy heart,
Why sigh'st thou without breaking?
where he answers again
Because thou canst not ease thy smart
By friendship nor by speaking.
There was never a truer rhyme. Let us cast away nothing, for we
may live to have need of such a verse. We see it, we see it. How
now, lambs!

*What a sight this is! Let me be hugged too.*
*'Oh heart,' as the proverb has it,*
*'O heart, heavy heart,*
*why do you sigh without breaking?*
*And he answers*
*because you cannot ease your pain*
*with friendship or with talk.'*
*There was never a truer song. Let's not throw anything away, for we*
*may need a verse such as this someday. I've seen it happen. What*
*shall you do, lambs!*

TROILUS.
Cressid, I love thee in so strain'd a purity
That the bless'd gods, as angry with my fancy,
More bright in zeal than the devotion which
Cold lips blow to their deities, take thee from me.

*Cressida, Ilove you in such a pure way*
*that the blessed gods, angry with my love,*
*because it is brighter than the prayers*
*they get from cold lips, are taking you from me.*

CRESSIDA.
Have the gods envy?

*Are the gods jealous?*

PANDARUS.
Ay, ay, ay; 'tis too plain a case.

*Yes, yes, yes; it's obvious.*

CRESSIDA.
And is it true that I must go from Troy?

*And is it true that I must leave Troy?*

TROILUS.
A hateful truth.

*A horrible truth.*

CRESSIDA.
What, and from Troilus too?

*What, and leave Troilus as well?*

TROILUS.
From Troy and Troilus.

*You must leave Troy and Troilus.*

CRESSIDA.
Is't possible?

*Is this really happening?*

TROILUS.
And suddenly; where injury of chance
Puts back leave-taking, justles roughly by
All time of pause, rudely beguiles our lips
Of all rejoindure, forcibly prevents
Our lock'd embrasures, strangles our dear vows
Even in the birth of our own labouring breath.
We two, that with so many thousand sighs
Did buy each other, must poorly sell ourselves
With the rude brevity and discharge of one.
Injurious time now with a robber's haste
Crams his rich thievery up, he knows not how.
As many farewells as be stars in heaven,
With distinct breath and consign'd kisses to them,
He fumbles up into a loose adieu,
And scants us with a single famish'd kiss,
Distasted with the salt of broken tears.

*It is, and suddenly; where bad luck*
*prevents saying goodbye, pushes roughly through*
*any delay, rudely blocks the chance of our lips*
*ever meeting again, violently stops*
*our intertwined embraces, strangles our precious vows*
*even as we say them.*
*We two, who spent so many thousand sighs*
*on each other, must now split*
*with time for only one.*
*Harmful Time now shoves all his plunder in a bag*
*with the haste of a burglar, any old way.*
*As many goodbyes as there are stars in heaven,*
*each one with its own words and kisses,*
*he screws them all up into a careless farewell*
*and rations us to a single hungry kiss,*
*whose taste is ruined with the salt of sobbing tears.*

AENEAS.
[Within] My lord, is the lady ready?

*My lord, is the lady ready?*

TROILUS.
Hark! you are call'd. Some say the Genius so
Cries 'Come' to him that instantly must die.
Bid them have patience; she shall come anon.

*Listen! They are calling you. Some say your guardian angel*
*calls 'come' like that to someone who is about to die.*
*Tell them to be patient; she'll be coming soon.*

PANDARUS.
Where are my tears? Rain, to lay this wind, or my heart
will be blown up by th' root.

*Where are my tears? I need rain to calm this wind, or my heart*
*will be torn up by the roots.*

Exit

CRESSIDA.
I must then to the Grecians?

*So I must go to the Greeks?*

TROILUS.
No remedy.

*There's no alternative.*

CRESSIDA.
A woeful Cressid 'mongst the merry Greeks!
When shall we see again?

*What an unhappy Cressida amongst the merry Greeks!*
*When shall we meet again?*

TROILUS.
Hear me, my love. Be thou but true of heart-

*Listen to me, my love. If you just remain faithful -*

CRESSIDA.
I true! how now! What wicked deem is this?

*Me faithful! What's this? What wicked thoughts are you having?*

TROILUS.
Nay, we must use expostulation kindly,
For it is parting from us.
I speak not 'Be thou true' as fearing thee,
For I will throw my glove to Death himself
That there's no maculation in thy heart;
But 'Be thou true' say I to fashion in
My sequent protestation: be thou true,
And I will see thee.

*No, we must discuss this calmly,*
*as soon we won't have the chance.*
*I didn't say "be faithful" because I doubted you,*
*for I would take on Death himself*
*to prove you have no inconstancy;*
*I say, "Be faithful" to lead into*
*what I was going to say: be faithful*
*and I will see you.*

CRESSIDA.

O, you shall be expos'd, my lord, to dangers
As infinite as imminent! But I'll be true.

*Oh, my lord, you will be exposed to dangers*
*as great as they will be swift!But I will be faithful.*

TROILUS.
And I'll grow friend with danger. Wear this sleeve.

*And I'll welcome the danger.Wear this cuff.*

CRESSIDA.
And you this glove. When shall I see you?

*And you wear this glove.When will I see you?*

TROILUS.
I will corrupt the Grecian sentinels
To give thee nightly visitation.
But yet be true.

*I'll bribe the Greek sentries*
*to let me see you every night.*
*But still be faithful.*

CRESSIDA.
O heavens! 'Be true' again!

*Oh heavens, 'be faithful' again!*

TROILUS.
Hear why I speak it, love.
The Grecian youths are full of quality;
They're loving, well compos'd with gifts of nature,
And flowing o'er with arts and exercise.
How novelties may move, and parts with person,
Alas, a kind of godly jealousy,
Which I beseech you call a virtuous sin,
Makes me afeard.

*Listen to why I say it, love.*
*The Greek youths are full of good breeding;*
*they're loving, nice looking,*
*and full of well practised skills.*

*The way new things can interest one, combined*
*with personal attractiveness, starts a kind*
*of divine jealously in me, which*
*makes me worried;*
*I hope you'll call this a good sin.*

CRESSIDA.
O heavens! you love me not.

*Oh heavens! You don't love me.*

TROILUS.
Die I a villain, then!
In this I do not call your faith in question
So mainly as my merit. I cannot sing,
Nor heel the high lavolt, nor sweeten talk,
Nor play at subtle games-fair virtues all,
To which the Grecians are most prompt and pregnant;
But I can tell that in each grace of these
There lurks a still and dumb-discoursive devil
That tempts most cunningly. But be not tempted.

*Then may I die as a villain!*
*I'm not calling your fidelity into question*
*as much as my virtues. I can't sing,*
*or dance fashionable dances, or talk sweetly,*
*nor play games which require skill - these are all good accomplishments,*
*which the Greeks are extremely good at;*
*and I know that in each of them*
*there is lurking a silent but persuasive devil*
*that tempts very cunningly. But don't be tempted.*

CRESSIDA.
Do you think I will?

*Do you think I will be?*

TROILUS.
No.
But something may be done that we will not;
And sometimes we are devils to ourselves,
When we will tempt the frailty of our powers,
Presuming on their changeful potency.

*No.*
*But sometimes things happen we don't want;*
*sometimes we are devils to ourselves,*
*when we rely to much on our own strength,*
*not realising we are all too unreliable.*

AENEAS.
[Within] Nay, good my lord!

*Enough, my good lord!*

TROILUS.
Come, kiss; and let us part.

*Come, kiss and let us part.*

PARIS.
[Within] Brother Troilus!

*Brother Troilus!*

TROILUS.
Good brother, come you hither;
And bring Aeneas and the Grecian with you.

*Good brother, come here;*
*and bring Aeneas and the Greek with you.*

CRESSIDA.
My lord, will you be true?

*My lord, will you be true?*

TROILUS.
Who, I? Alas, it is my vice, my fault!
Whiles others fish with craft for great opinion,
I with great truth catch mere simplicity;
Whilst some with cunning gild their copper crowns,
With truth and plainness I do wear mine bare.
Enter AENEAS, PARIS, ANTENOR, DEIPHOBUS, and DIOMEDES
Fear not my truth: the moral of my wit
Is 'plain and true'; there's all the reach of it.
Welcome, Sir Diomed! Here is the lady
Which for Antenor we deliver you;

At the port, lord, I'll give her to thy hand,
And by the way possess thee what she is.
Entreat her fair; and, by my soul, fair Greek,
If e'er thou stand at mercy of my sword,
Name Cressid, and thy life shall be as safe
As Priam is in Ilion.

*Who, me? Alas, it is a vice, a fault of mine.*
*While others cunningly try to gain a great reputation,*
*I get a reputation for being plain and simple through truthfulness;*
*while some craftily cover their copper crowns with gold,*
*I wear mine ungilded in truth and plainness.*

*Don't worry about my fidelity. My character can be summed up*
*as 'plain and true'; that's all there is to it–*
*Welcome, Sir Diomedes. Here is the lady*
*which we are exchanging with you for Antenor.*
*At the city gate, lord, I will hand her over to you,*
*and on the way I'll tell you about who she is.*
*Treat her well and I swear, fair Greek,*
*that if I ever have you at swordpoint.*
*just mention Cressida, and you'll be as safe*
*as Priam is in Ilium.*

DIOMEDES.
Fair Lady Cressid,
So please you, save the thanks this prince expects.
The lustre in your eye, heaven in your cheek,
Pleads your fair usage; and to Diomed
You shall be mistress, and command him wholly.

*Fair Lady Cressida,*
*if you please, you don't have to thank this prince.*
*Your shining eyes, your white cheek,*
*tell me to treat you well; you shall be*
*my mistress, I'm completely at your command.*

TROILUS.
Grecian, thou dost not use me courteously
To shame the zeal of my petition to thee
In praising her. I tell thee, lord of Greece,
She is as far high-soaring o'er thy praises
As thou unworthy to be call'd her servant.
I charge thee use her well, even for my charge;

For, by the dreadful Pluto, if thou dost not,
Though the great bulk Achilles be thy guard,
I'll cut thy throat.

*Greek, you're not being polite*
*by putting down the sincerity of my request*
*by praising her. I tell you, Lord of Greece,*
*she is as high above your praises*
*as you are unworthy to be called her servant.*
*I order you to treat her well, just because I tell you to;*
*for, I swear by dreadful Pluto, if you don't,*
*if the great body of Achilles was guarding you,*
*I'll cut your throat.*

DIOMEDES.
O, be not mov'd, Prince Troilus.
Let me be privileg'd by my place and message
To be a speaker free: when I am hence
I'll answer to my lust. And know you, lord,
I'll nothing do on charge: to her own worth
She shall be priz'd. But that you say 'Be't so,'
I speak it in my spirit and honour, 'No.'

*Oh, don't be upset, Prince Troilus.*
*Allow me to use the privilege of my position*
*to speak freely. When I have gone*
*I'll do what I wish. And you should know, Lord,*
*I don't accept orders: she shall be treated well*
*because of her own worth; but absolutely not*
*because you've told me to.*

TROILUS.
Come, to the port. I'll tell thee, Diomed,
This brave shall oft make thee to hide thy head.
Lady, give me your hand; and, as we walk,
To our own selves bend we our needful talk.

*Come, to the gate. I tell you, Diomedes,*
*this boasting will backfire on you one day.*
*Lady, give me your hand; and, as we walk,*
*let's just talk to each other.*

Exeunt TROILUS, CRESSIDA, and DIOMEDES
[Sound trumpet]

---

PARIS.
Hark! Hector's trumpet.

*Hear that! Hector's trumpet.*

AENEAS.
How have we spent this morning!
The Prince must think me tardy and remiss,
That swore to ride before him to the field.

*How has all this time gone by!*
*The prince must think I am late and negligent,*
*I promised I would ride ahead of him on the battlefield.*

PARIS.
'Tis Troilus' fault. Come, come to field with him.

*It's Troilus' fault. Come, come to the battlefield with him.*

DEIPHOBUS.
Let us make ready straight.

*Let's get ready at once.*

AENEAS.
Yea, with a bridegroom's fresh alacrity
Let us address to tend on Hector's heels.
The glory of our Troy doth this day lie
On his fair worth and single chivalry.

*Yes, with the keenness of a bridegroom,*
*let's set ourselves to walk in Hector's footsteps.*
*The glory of Troy today rests*
*on his great honour and single combat.*

Exeunt

## SCENE 5. The Grecian camp. Lists set out

Enter AJAX, armed; AGAMEMNON, ACHILLES, PATROCLUS, MENELAUS,

ULYSSES, NESTOR, and others

AGAMEMNON.
Here art thou in appointment fresh and fair,
Anticipating time with starting courage.
Give with thy trumpet a loud note to Troy,
Thou dreadful Ajax, that the appalled air
May pierce the head of the great combatant,
And hale him hither.

*Here you are in your spick and span equipment,*
*ready to go with eager courage.*
*Blow a loud note on your trumpet for Troy,*
*awe-inspiring Ajax, so that the terrifying sound*
*can drive into the head of the great fighter,*
*and call him here.*

AJAX.
Thou, trumpet, there's my purse.
Now crack thy lungs and split thy brazen pipe;
Blow, villain, till thy sphered bias cheek
Out-swell the colic of puff Aquilon'd.
Come, stretch thy chest, and let thy eyes spout blood:
Thou blowest for Hector. [Trumpet sounds]

*You, trumpeter, here's your fee.*
*Now crack your lungs and burst your brass trumpet open;*
*blow, scoundrel, until your blown out cheeks*
*excel those of the North wind.*
*Come, fill up your lungs, and let your eyes spout blood:*
*you're blowing for Hector.*

ULYSSES.
No trumpet answers.

*There's no answering trumpet.*

ACHILLES.
'Tis but early days.

*It's early days.*

Enter DIOMEDES, with CRESSIDA

AGAMEMNON.
Is not yond Diomed, with Calchas' daughter?

*Isn't that Diomedes over there, with Calchas' daughter?*

ULYSSES.
'Tis he, I ken the manner of his gait:
He rises on the toe. That spirit of his
In aspiration lifts him from the earth.

*It's him, I know the way he walks:*
*he walks on the balls of his feet. His great spirit*
*lifts him above the earth.*

AGAMEMNON.
Is this the lady Cressid?

*Is that the lady Cressida?*

DIOMEDES.
Even she.

*That's the one.*

AGAMEMNON.
Most dearly welcome to the Greeks, sweet lady.

*The Greeks give you a warm welcome, sweet lady.*

NESTOR.
Our general doth salute you with a kiss.

*Our general greets you with a kiss.*

ULYSSES.
Yet is the kindness but particular;

'Twere better she were kiss'd in general.

*But that's just an individual kindness;*
*it would be better if she were generally kissed.*

NESTOR.
And very courtly counsel: I'll begin.
So much for Nestor.

*Very gallant advice: I'll go first.*
*Nestor is done.*

ACHILLES.
I'll take that winter from your lips, fair lady.
Achilles bids you welcome.

*I'll take the chill of the old man off your lips, fair Lady.*
*Achilles welcomes you.*

MENELAUS.
I had good argument for kissing once.

*I once had a good subject for kissing.*

PATROCLUS.
But that's no argument for kissing now;
For thus popp'd Paris in his hardiment,
And parted thus you and your argument.

*But that's no reason for you to kiss now;*
*for up popped hard bold Paris,*
*and split you from your subject.*

ULYSSES.
O deadly gall, and theme of all our scorns!
For which we lose our heads to gild his horns.

*What a terrible business, which makes a mockery of us!*
*We're being killed to put a better gloss on the fact that he's been cheated on.*

PATROCLUS.
The first was Menelaus' kiss; this, mine-
[Kisses her again]
Patroclus kisses you.

186

*That first kiss belonged to Menelaus; this one's for me–*
*[kisses her again]*
*Patroclus kisses you.*

MENELAUS.
O, this is trim!

*Oh, this is a fine thing!*

PATROCLUS.
Paris and I kiss evermore for him.

*Paris and I do his kissing for him now.*

MENELAUS.
I'll have my kiss, sir. Lady, by your leave.

*I shall have my kiss, sir. Lady, with your permission.*

CRESSIDA.
In kissing, do you render or receive?

*In kissing, are you giving or receiving?*

PATROCLUS.
Both take and give.

*Both taking and giving.*

CRESSIDA.
I'll make my match to live,
The kiss you take is better than you give;
Therefore no kiss.

*I'll bet my life,*
*the kiss you take is better than the one you give;*
*so no kiss for you.*

MENELAUS.
I'll give you boot; I'll give you three for one.

*I'll give you odds; I'll give you three for one.*

CRESSIDA.
You are an odd man; give even or give none.

*You are an odd man; match what you get or don't give at all.*

MENELAUS.
An odd man, lady? Every man is odd.

*An odd man, lady? Every man is odd.*

CRESSIDA.
No, Paris is not; for you know 'tis true
That you are odd, and he is even with you.

*No, Paris is not; you know it's true*
*that you are odd, and he is quits with you.*

MENELAUS.
You fillip me o' th' head.

*You're touching a sensitive spot.*

CRESSIDA.
No, I'll be sworn.

*No, I swear not.*

ULYSSES.
It were no match, your nail against his horn.
May I, sweet lady, beg a kiss of you?

*It wasn't a fair fight, your nail against his horn.*
*May I, sweet lady, ask you for a kiss?*

CRESSIDA.
You may.

*You may.*

ULYSSES.
I do desire it.

*I desire it.*

CRESSIDA.
Why, beg then.

*Well then, beg.*

ULYSSES.
Why then, for Venus' sake give me a kiss
When Helen is a maid again, and his.

*Well then, for the sake of love, give me a kiss*
*when Helen is in her proper place as his wife—*

CRESSIDA.
I am your debtor; claim it when 'tis due.

*I owe it to you; claim it when it's due.*

ULYSSES.
Never's my day, and then a kiss of you.

*It seems I'll never get that kiss then.*

DIOMEDES.
Lady, a word. I'll bring you to your father.

*Lady, a word. I'll take you to your father.*

Exit with CRESSIDA

NESTOR.
A woman of quick sense.

*A quickwitted woman.*

ULYSSES.
Fie, fie upon her!
There's language in her eye, her cheek, her lip,
Nay, her foot speaks; her wanton spirits look out
At every joint and motive of her body.
O these encounters so glib of tongue
That give a coasting welcome ere it comes,
And wide unclasp the tables of their thoughts
To every ticklish reader! Set them down
For sluttish spoils of opportunity,

And daughters of the game. [Trumpet within]

*Damnation to her!*
*You can read things in her eye, her cheeks, her lips,*
*even her foot speaks; her lusty spirit is shown*
*in every joint and movement of her body.*
*Oh, these forward women, so clever with their tongue,*
*that make advances to men before they've even offered,*
*and open up themselves like books*
*to every curious reader! Put them down*
*as sluttish women who can be had any time,*
*no better than prostitutes.*

ALL.
The Troyans' trumpet.

*The Trojans' trumpet.*

Enter HECTOR, armed; AENEAS, TROILUS, PARIS, HELENUS,
and other Trojans, with attendants

AGAMEMNON.
Yonder comes the troop.

*Here comes the troop.*

AENEAS.
Hail, all the state of Greece! What shall be done
To him that victory commands? Or do you purpose
A victor shall be known? Will you the knights
Shall to the edge of all extremity
Pursue each other, or shall they be divided
By any voice or order of the field?
Hector bade ask.

*Greetings, rulers of Greece! What shall be given*
*to the winner? Do you intend*
*that a winner should be chosen? Do you wish for the knights*
*to fight each other to the death,*
*or should they be separated*
*by some umpire or by the laws of chivalry?*
*Hector told me to ask this.*

AGAMEMNON.

Which way would Hector have it?

*Which way does Hector want it?*

AENEAS.
He cares not; he'll obey conditions.

*He doesn't care; he'll follow whatever's agreed on.*

ACHILLES.
'Tis done like Hector; but securely done,
A little proudly, and great deal misprizing
The knight oppos'd.

*This is done like Hector; over confidently,
rather arrogantly, and very much disparaging
his opponent.*

AENEAS.
If not Achilles, sir,
What is your name?

*If you are not Achilles, Sir,
what is your name?*

ACHILLES.
If not Achilles, nothing.

*If I'm not Achilles, then I don't have a name.*

AENEAS.
Therefore Achilles. But whate'er, know this:
In the extremity of great and little
Valour and pride excel themselves in Hector;
The one almost as infinite as all,
The other blank as nothing. Weigh him well,
And that which looks like pride is courtesy.
This Ajax is half made of Hector's blood;
In love whereof half Hector stays at home;
Half heart, half hand, half Hector comes to seek
This blended knight, half Troyan and half Greek.

*So you are Achilles. But whatever you are, know this:
in Hector bravery and arrogance are shown at*

*absolutely opposite extremes;*
*bravery that is almost infinite,*
*and not a drop of pride. If you look closely*
*what looks like pride is courtesy.*
*This Ajax shares half of Hector's ancestry;*
*out of respect for that half of Hector stays at home;*
*half a heart, half a hand, half of Hector comes to find*
*thisblended knight, half Trojan and half Greek.*

ACHILLES.
A maiden battle then? O, I perceive you!

*Oh, I see! This is to be a battle without bloodshed?*

Re-enter DIOMEDES

AGAMEMNON.
Here is Sir Diomed. Go, gentle knight,
Stand by our Ajax. As you and Lord Aeneas
Consent upon the order of their fight,
So be it; either to the uttermost,
Or else a breath. The combatants being kin
Half stints their strife before their strokes begin.

*Here is Sir Diomedes. Go, gentle knight,*
*stand next to our Ajax. As you and Lord Aeneas*
*agree on the procedure for their fight,*
*that's how it will be; either to the death,*
*or else just for exercise. The combatants being related*
*cuts short their fight before they even start.*

[AJAX and HECTOR enter the lists]

ULYSSES.
They are oppos'd already.

*They are already squaring up.*

AGAMEMNON.
What Troyan is that same that looks so heavy?

*Who's that Trojan who looks so depressed?*

ULYSSES.

The youngest son of Priam, a true knight;
Not yet mature, yet matchless; firm of word;
Speaking in deeds and deedless in his tongue;
Not soon provok'd, nor being provok'd soon calm'd;
His heart and hand both open and both free;
For what he has he gives, what thinks he shows,
Yet gives he not till judgment guide his bounty,
Nor dignifies an impair thought with breath;
Manly as Hector, but more dangerous;
For Hector in his blaze of wrath subscribes
To tender objects, but he in heat of action
Is more vindicative than jealous love.
They call him Troilus, and on him erect
A second hope as fairly built as Hector.
Thus says Aeneas, one that knows the youth
Even to his inches, and, with private soul,
Did in great Ilion thus translate him to me.

*The youngest son of Priam, a true knight;*
*not fully grown, but matchless; true to his word;*
*speaking through his deeds but never boastful;*
*not quick to anger, but not quick to calm down when angry;*
*he's generous with money and with his love;*
*what he has he gives, what he thinks he shows,*
*though he gives sensibly,*
*and never speaks an impure thought;*
*he's as manly as Hector, but more dangerous;*
*for Hector will give mercy to the defenceless*
*even in the heat of his anger, but he in the heat of action*
*is more vindictive than a jealous lover.*
*They call him Troilus, and they pin their hopes on him,*
*second only to Hector, and just as well built.*
*That's what Aeneas has said, someone who knows*
*every inch of the lad, and he privately and from the heart*
*described him to me in these terms when we were in Troy.*

[Alarum. HECTOR and AJAX fight]

AGAMEMNON.
They are in action.

*They have begun.*

NESTOR.

Now, Ajax, hold thine own!

*Now, Ajax, stand your ground!*

TROILUS.
Hector, thou sleep'st;
Awake thee.

*Hector, you're asleep;*
*wake up.*

AGAMEMNON.
His blows are well dispos'd. There, Ajax!

*His blows are well placed. Well done, Ajax!*

[Trumpets cease]

DIOMEDES.
You must no more.

*You mustn't carry on.*

AENEAS.
Princes, enough, so please you.

*Princes, that's enough, please.*

AJAX.
I am not warm yet; let us fight again.

*I haven't broken sweat; let's fight again.*

DIOMEDES.
As Hector pleases.

*It's up to Hector.*

HECTOR.
Why, then will I no more.
Thou art, great lord, my father's sister's son,
A cousin-german to great Priam's seed;
The obligation of our blood forbids
A gory emulation 'twixt us twain:

———

194

Were thy commixtion Greek and Troyan so
That thou could'st say 'This hand is Grecian all,
And this is Troyan; the sinews of this leg
All Greek, and this all Troy; my mother's blood
Runs on the dexter cheek, and this sinister
Bounds in my father's'; by Jove multipotent,
Thou shouldst not bear from me a Greekish member
Wherein my sword had not impressure made
Of our rank feud; but the just gods gainsay
That any drop thou borrow'dst from thy mother,
My sacred aunt, should by my mortal sword
Be drained! Let me embrace thee, Ajax.
By him that thunders, thou hast lusty arms;
Hector would have them fall upon him thus.
Cousin, all honour to thee!

*Well, then I won't fight any more.*
*You, great lord, are my father's sister's son,*
*first cousin to the family of great Priam;*
*the ties of our blood forbid us*
*to participate in bloody rivalry:*
*if your mixture of Greek and Trojan was such*
*that one could say, 'This hand is all Greek,*
*and this is Trojan; the muscles of this leg*
*are all Greek, and this is all Trojan; my mother's blood*
*runs in the right cheek, and the left*
*is full of my father's'; by omnipotent Jove,*
*you wouldn't walk away with any Greek limbs*
*which didn't have the mark of my sword on them;*
*but the just gods forbid*
*that any blood which you had from your mother,*
*my sacred aunt, should be spilt by my sword.*
*Let me embrace you, Ajax.*
*By Jove, you have strong arms;*
*Hector wants them to fall upon him this way.*
*Cousin, all honour to you!*

AJAX.
I thank thee, Hector.
Thou art too gentle and too free a man.
I came to kill thee, cousin, and bear hence
A great addition earned in thy death.

*I thank you, Hector.*

*You are too tender and too generous a man.*
*I came to kill you, cousin, and carry away*
*a great title earned by your death.*

HECTOR.
Not Neoptolemus so mirable,
On whose bright crest Fame with her loud'st Oyes
Cries 'This is he' could promise to himself
A thought of added honour torn from Hector.

*Not even great Achilles,*
*on whose bright shield fame cries out loudly*
*'This is the one' could be confident of*
*getting honour by tearing it away from Hector.*

AENEAS.
There is expectance here from both the sides
What further you will do.

*Everyone here on both sides*
*wants to know what you will do next.*

HECTOR.
We'll answer it:
The issue is embracement. Ajax, farewell.

*We'll tell them:*
*what we shall do is embrace. Ajax, farewell.*

AJAX.
If I might in entreaties find success,
As seld I have the chance, I would desire
My famous cousin to our Grecian tents.

*If my pleading might be answered,*
*since I rarely get the chance, I should like*
*my famous cousin to visit our Greek tents.*

DIOMEDES.
'Tis Agamemnon's wish; and great Achilles
Doth long to see unarm'd the valiant Hector.

*That's what Agamemnon wants; and great Achilles*
*longs to see the valiant Hector away from the battlefield.*

---

HECTOR.
Aeneas, call my brother Troilus to me,
And signify this loving interview
To the expecters of our Troyan part;
Desire them home. Give me thy hand, my cousin;
I will go eat with thee, and see your knights.

*Aeneas, call my brother Troilus to me,*
*and tell those Trojans waiting for news*
*about this friendly conversation;*
*tell them to go home. Give me your hand, my cousin;*
*I will go and eat with you, and see your knights.*

AGAMEMNON and the rest of the Greeks come forward

AJAX.
Great Agamemnon comes to meet us here.

*Great Agamemnon has come to meet us.*

HECTOR.
The worthiest of them tell me name by name;
But for Achilles, my own searching eyes
Shall find him by his large and portly size.

*Name all the best of them to me;*
*but as for Achilles, my own eyes*
*shall recognise him due to his size and dignity.*

AGAMEMNON.
Worthy all arms! as welcome as to one
That would be rid of such an enemy.
But that's no welcome. Understand more clear,
What's past and what's to come is strew'd with husks
And formless ruin of oblivion;
But in this extant moment, faith and troth,
Strain'd purely from all hollow bias-drawing,
Bids thee with most divine integrity,
From heart of very heart, great Hector, welcome.

*You deserve your arms! You are as welcome as it's possible to be*
*to someone who is fighting as your enemy.*
*But that's no welcome. Let me make it more clear,*

*the past and the future are full of the remains*
*of great achievements, now in ruins;*
*but at this very moment, trustworthiness and honesty,*
*free of any cunning or strategy,*
*says to you with godlike integrity,*
*from the very bottom of my heart, great Hector, welcome.*

HECTOR.
I thank thee, most imperious Agamemnon.

*I thank you, most imperial Agamemnon.*

AGAMEMNON.
[To Troilus] My well-fam'd lord of Troy, no less to you.

*You famous lord of Troy, no less to you.*

MENELAUS.
Let me confirm my princely brother's greeting.
You brace of warlike brothers, welcome hither.

*Let me second the greetings of my princely brother.*
*You pair of warlike brothers, you are welcome here.*

HECTOR.
Who must we answer?

*Who is this?*

AENEAS.
The noble Menelaus.

*The noble Menelaus.*

HECTOR.
O you, my lord? By Mars his gauntlet, thanks!
Mock not that I affect the untraded oath;
Your quondam wife swears still by Venus' glove.
She's well, but bade me not commend her to you.

*Oh it's you, my lord? Thank you, by the armoured glove of Mars!*
*Don't mock me for inventing new oaths;*
*your former wife still swears by the glove of Venus.*
*She's well, but she didn't ask me to remember her to you.*

198

MENELAUS.
Name her not now, sir; she's a deadly theme.

*Don't speak of her now, sir; she's a miserable subject.*

HECTOR.
O, pardon; I offend.

*I'm sorry; I've upset you.*

NESTOR.
I have, thou gallant Troyan, seen thee oft,
Labouring for destiny, make cruel way
Through ranks of Greekish youth; and I have seen thee,
As hot as Perseus, spur thy Phrygian steed,
Despising many forfeits and subduements,
When thou hast hung thy advanced sword i' th' air,
Not letting it decline on the declined;
That I have said to some my standers-by
'Lo, Jupiter is yonder, dealing life!'
And I have seen thee pause and take thy breath,
When that a ring of Greeks have hemm'd thee in,
Like an Olympian wrestling. This have I seen;
But this thy countenance, still lock'd in steel,
I never saw till now. I knew thy grandsire,
And once fought with him. He was a soldier good,
But, by great Mars, the captain of us all,
Never like thee. O, let an old man embrace thee;
And, worthy warrior, welcome to our tents.

*I have often seen you, gallant Trojan,*
*working for fate, cutting your way*
*through the ranks of young Greeks; and I have seen you,*
*as eager as Perseus, spur on your Trojan horse,*
*refusing to take advantage of those at your mercy,*
*checking the swing of your raised sword,*
*not letting it fall on the fallen;*
*so I have said to some of my hangers on,*
*'Look, there is Jupiter, giving out life!'*
*And I have seen you pause and catch your breath,*
*when a ring of Greeks have surrounded you,*
*like a wrestler in the Olympic Games. I have seen this;*
*but your face was always covered with your helmet,*

*I never saw it until now. I knew your grandfather,*
*and once fought with him. He was a good soldier,*
*but, I swear by great Mars, the captain of us all,*
*he was never like you. O, let an old man embrace you;*
*and, worthy warrior, welcome to our camp.*

AENEAS.
'Tis the old Nestor.

*This is old Nestor.*

HECTOR.
Let me embrace thee, good old chronicle,
That hast so long walk'd hand in hand with time.
Most reverend Nestor, I am glad to clasp thee.

*Let me embrace you, good old memory house,*
*who has lived so long.*
*Most respected Nestor, I am glad to embrace you.*

NESTOR.
I would my arms could match thee in contention
As they contend with thee in courtesy.

*I wish my arms could match you in battle*
*as they are matched with you in politeness.*

HECTOR.
I would they could.

*I wish they could.*

NESTOR.
Ha!
By this white beard, I'd fight with thee to-morrow.
Well, welcome, welcome! I have seen the time.

*Ha!*
*If it wasn't for this white beard, I'd fight with you tomorrow.*
*Well, welcome, welcome! There was a time when I would have taken you on.*

ULYSSES.
I wonder now how yonder city stands,
When we have here her base and pillar by us.

*I wonder how that city is still standing,*
*when we have her foundations and support with us.*

HECTOR.
I know your favour, Lord Ulysses, well.
Ah, sir, there's many a Greek and Troyan dead,
Since first I saw yourself and Diomed
In Ilion on your Greekish embassy.

*I know your face, Lord Ulysses, well.*
*Ah, sir, there have been many Greeks and Trojans killed,*
*since I first saw you and Diomedes*
*in Troy on your Greek embassy.*

ULYSSES.
Sir, I foretold you then what would ensue.
My prophecy is but half his journey yet;
For yonder walls, that pertly front your town,
Yond towers, whose wanton tops do buss the clouds,
Must kiss their own feet.

*Sir, I predicted to you then what would happen.*
*my prophecy is only half fulfilled;*
*for those walls, which bravely surround your town,*
*those towers, whose insolent tops kiss the clouds,*
*will come down.*

HECTOR.
I must not believe you.
There they stand yet; and modestly I think
The fall of every Phrygian stone will cost
A drop of Grecian blood. The end crowns all;
And that old common arbitrator, Time,
Will one day end it.

*I will not believe you.*
*They are still standing there; and without exaggeration*
*I think that every Trojan stone which falls will cost*
*a drop of Greek blood. We'll see what happens in the end;*
*and the old common umpire, Time,*
*will end it one day.*

ULYSSES.

So to him we leave it.
Most gentle and most valiant Hector, welcome.
After the General, I beseech you next
To feast with me and see me at my tent.

*So we'll leave it to him.*
*Most noble and most valiant Hector, welcome.*
*After you've seen the general, I beg you*
*to come and feast with me at my tent.*

ACHILLES.
I shall forestall thee, Lord Ulysses, thou!
Now, Hector, I have fed mine eyes on thee;
I have with exact view perus'd thee, Hector,
And quoted joint by joint.

*I shall get in ahead of you, Lord Ulysses!*
*Now, Hector, I have looked closely at you;*
*I have carefully looked over*
*every inch of you, Hector.*

HECTOR.
Is this Achilles?

*Is this Achilles?*

ACHILLES.
I am Achilles.

*I am Achilles.*

HECTOR.
Stand fair, I pray thee; let me look on thee.

*Stand in plain view, I beg you; let me look at you.*

ACHILLES.
Behold thy fill.

*Look all you want.*

HECTOR.
Nay, I have done already.

*No, I'm finished.*

ACHILLES.
Thou art too brief. I will the second time,
As I would buy thee, view thee limb by limb.

*You're too swift. I will have a look over you*
*limb by limb, as if I was going to buy you.*

HECTOR.
O, like a book of sport thou'lt read me o'er;
But there's more in me than thou understand'st.
Why dost thou so oppress me with thine eye?

*Oh you'll read me like a huntsman's handbook;*
*but there's more to me than you understand.*
*Why are you glaring at me like that?*

ACHILLES.
Tell me, you heavens, in which part of his body
Shall I destroy him? Whether there, or there, or there?
That I may give the local wound a name,
And make distinct the very breach whereout
Hector's great spirit flew. Answer me, heavens.

*Tell me, you heavens, where on his body*
*shall I strike the killer blow? There, or there, or there?*
*I want to know the exact spot,*
*and mark out exactly where*
*Hector's great soul flew out. Answer me, heavens.*

HECTOR.
It would discredit the blest gods, proud man,
To answer such a question. Stand again.
Think'st thou to catch my life so pleasantly
As to prenominate in nice conjecture
Where thou wilt hit me dead?

*It would be unworthy of the great gods, arrogant man,*
*to answer a question like that. Get back on your feet.*
*You think it's going to be so easy to kill me*
*that you can nominate beforehand*
*where you will put the deadly blow?*

ACHILLES.
I tell thee yea.

*I'm telling you, yes.*

HECTOR.
Wert thou an oracle to tell me so,
I'd not believe thee. Henceforth guard thee well;
For I'll not kill thee there, nor there, nor there;
But, by the forge that stithied Mars his helm,
I'll kill thee everywhere, yea, o'er and o'er.
You wisest Grecians, pardon me this brag.
His insolence draws folly from my lips;
But I'll endeavour deeds to match these words,
Or may I never-

*If you were an Oracle telling me this,*
*I wouldn't believe you. From now on be on your guard;*
*for I won't kill you there, nor there, nor there;*
*but, I swear by the forge that made Mars' helmet,*
*I'll kill you everywhere, yes, over and over.*
*You wisest Greeks, excuse my boasting.*
*His insolence makes me say foolish things.*
*But I'll try to match my words with deeds,*
*or may I never–*

AJAX.
Do not chafe thee, cousin;
And you, Achilles, let these threats alone
Till accident or purpose bring you to't.
You may have every day enough of Hector,
If you have stomach. The general state, I fear,
Can scarce entreat you to be odd with him.

*Don't to be angry, cousin.*
*And you, Achilles, stop making these threats,*
*until, accidentally or on purpose, you two meet in combat.*
*You can fight with Hector every day,*
*if you have the stomach for it. The Greek commanders, I'm afraid,*
*can't persuade you to be so confrontational with him.*

HECTOR.
I pray you let us see you in the field;
We have had pelting wars since you refus'd

The Grecians' cause.

*I ask you, let us see you on the battlefield.*
*The battles have been insignificant since you refused*
*to fight for the Greeks.*

ACHILLES.
Dost thou entreat me, Hector?
To-morrow do I meet thee, fell as death;
To-night all friends.

*Are you inviting me, Hector?*
*Tomorrow I shall meet you, fierce as death;*
*tonight we'll all be friends.*

HECTOR.
Thy hand upon that match.

*Shake hands on that.*

AGAMEMNON.
First, all you peers of Greece, go to my tent;
There in the full convive we; afterwards,
As Hector's leisure and your bounties shall
Concur together, severally entreat him.
Beat loud the tambourines, let the trumpets blow,
That this great soldier may his welcome know.

*First, all you lords of Greece, go to my tent;*
*then we will have a great feast together. Afterwards,*
*depending on what Hector wants and you can offer him,*
*you can entertain him yourselves.*
*Play the tambourines loudly, let the trumpets blow,*
*to show this great soldier our welcome.*

Exeunt all but TROILUS and ULYSSES

TROILUS.
My Lord Ulysses, tell me, I beseech you,
In what place of the field doth Calchas keep?

*My Lord Ulysses, tell me, I beg you,*
*whereabouts in the camp does Calchas stay?*

ULYSSES.
At Menelaus' tent, most princely Troilus.
There Diomed doth feast with him to-night,
Who neither looks upon the heaven nor earth,
But gives all gaze and bent of amorous view
On the fair Cressid.

*At Menelaus' tent, most princely Troilus.*
*Diomedes is feasting with him there tonight,*
*who doesn't look at the earth or the skies,*
*but spends all his looks lovingly*
*on the beautiful Cressida.*

TROILUS.
Shall I, sweet lord, be bound to you so much,
After we part from Agamemnon's tent,
To bring me thither?

*Would you be so kind, sweet lord,*
*after we leave Agamemnon's tent,*
*to take me there?*

ULYSSES.
You shall command me, sir.
As gentle tell me of what honour was
This Cressida in Troy? Had she no lover there
That wails her absence?

*I'm at your disposal, sir.*
*Be so kind as to tell me what was this Cressida's*
*reputation in Troy? Did she have no lover there,*
*who is missing her?*

TROILUS.
O, sir, to such as boasting show their scars
A mock is due. Will you walk on, my lord?
She was belov'd, she lov'd; she is, and doth;
But still sweet love is food for fortune's tooth.

*Oh, sir, those who boast and show their scars*
*should be mocked. Will you walk on, my lord?*
*She was loved and loved in return; she still is, and does;*
*but still, sweet love is still the plaything of fate.*

Exeunt

# ACT V

# SCENE 1. The Grecian camp. Before the tent of ACHILLES

Enter ACHILLES and PATROCLUS

ACHILLES.
I'll heat his blood with Greekish wine to-night,
Which with my scimitar I'll cool to-morrow.
Patroclus, let us feast him to the height.

*I'll warm his blood with Greek wine tonight*
*and tomorrow I'll cool it down with my sword.*
*Patroclus, let's give him a great feast.*

PATROCLUS.
Here comes Thersites.

*Here comes Thersites.*

Enter THERSITES

ACHILLES.
How now, thou core of envy!
Thou crusty batch of nature, what's the news?

*Hello, you dregs of envy!*
*You scabby depraved object, what's the news?*

THERSITES.
Why, thou picture of what thou seemest, and idol of
idiot worshippers, here's a letter for thee.

*Why, you who are all show and no substance,*
*the idol of foolish worshippers, here's a letter for you.*

ACHILLES.
From whence, fragment?

*Where from, youdreg?*

THERSITES.

Why, thou full dish of fool, from Troy.

*Why you great bowlful of idiocy, from Troy.*

PATROCLUS.
Who keeps the tent now?

*Who's keeping to his tent now?*

THERSITES.
The surgeon's box or the patient's wound.

*The surgeon's box or the patient's wound.*

PATROCLUS.
Well said, Adversity! and what needs these tricks?

*Well said, perverse creature! Now what's the point in these word games?*

THERSITES.
Prithee, be silent, boy; I profit not by thy talk; thou
art said to be Achilles' male varlet.

*Please, be silent, boy; your talk is useless to me; you
are said to be Achilles' manservant.*

PATROCLUS.
Male varlet, you rogue! What's that?

*Manservant, you rogue! What's that mean?*

THERSITES.
Why, his masculine whore. Now, the rotten diseases of
the south, the guts-griping ruptures, catarrhs, loads o' gravel
in the back, lethargies, cold palsies, raw eyes, dirt-rotten
livers, wheezing lungs, bladders full of imposthume, sciaticas,
limekilns i' th' palm, incurable bone-ache, and the rivelled fee-
simple of the tetter, take and take again such preposterous
discoveries!

*Why, his masculine whore. Now, may the rotten diseases of
the South, colic, colds, shingles,
sleeping sickness, shakes, sore eyes, rotting
livers, wheezing lungs, bladders full of ulcers, sciatica,*

warts, rheumatism, and all the scars that boils leave
overcome such filthy inversions!

PATROCLUS.
Why, thou damnable box of envy, thou, what meanest thou
to curse thus?

*Why you dammed swine, what do you mean*
*by this curse?*

THERSITES.
Do I curse thee?

*Am I cursing you?*

PATROCLUS.
Why, no, you ruinous butt; you whoreson
indistinguishable cur, no.

*Why, no, you revolting ass; you son of a bitch mongrel*
*dog, no.*

THERSITES.
No! Why art thou, then, exasperate, thou idle immaterial
skein of sled silk, thou green sarcenet flap for a sore eye,
thou tassel of a prodigal's purse, thou? Ah, how the poor world is
pestered with such water-flies-diminutives of nature!

*No! Then why are upset, you idle useless piece of*
*embroidery silk, you flimsy green eyepatch for a sore eye,*
*you frilly decoration on a spendthrift's purse? Ah, how the poor world is*
*bothered by such mosquitoes–the tiny things of nature!*

PATROCLUS.
Out, gall!

*Get out, boil!*

THERSITES.
Finch egg!

*Speck!*

ACHILLES.

My sweet Patroclus, I am thwarted quite
From my great purpose in to-morrow's battle.
Here is a letter from Queen Hecuba,
A token from her daughter, my fair love,
Both taxing me and gaging me to keep
An oath that I have sworn. I will not break it.
Fall Greeks; fail fame; honour or go or stay;
My major vow lies here, this I'll obey.
Come, come, Thersites, help to trim my tent;
This night in banqueting must all be spent.
Away, Patroclus! Exit with PATROCLUS

*My sweet Patroclus, I have been quite diverted*
*from my plan for tomorrow's battle.*
*Here is a letter from Queen Hecuba,*
*a present from her daughter, my fair love,*
*both reproving me and reminding me to keep*
*an oath that I have sworn. I will not break it.*
*The Greeks can lose; fame can disappear; honour can come and go;*
*this is my greatest promise, this is what I shall obey.*
*Come, come, Thersites, help tidy my tent;*
*tonight will be spent banqueting.*
*Come on, Patroclus!*

THERSITES.
With too much blood and too little brain these two may
run mad; but, if with too much brain and to little blood they do,
I'll be a curer of madmen. Here's Agamemnon, an honest fellow
enough, and one that loves quails, but he has not so much brain
as ear-wax; and the goodly transformation of Jupiter there, his
brother, the bull, the primitive statue and oblique memorial of
cuckolds, a thrifty shoeing-horn in a chain, hanging at his
brother's leg-to what form but that he is, should wit larded with
malice, and malice forced with wit, turn him to? To an ass, were
nothing: he is both ass and ox. To an ox, were nothing: he is both
ox and ass. To be a dog, a mule, a cat, a fitchew, a toad, a
lizard, an owl, a put-tock, or a herring without a roe, I would
not care; but to be Menelaus, I would conspire against destiny.
Ask me not what I would be, if I were not Thersites; for I care
not to be the louse of a lazar, so I were not Menelaus. Hey-day!
sprites and fires!

*With too much passion and not enough brains these two may*
*go mad; but if they went mad with too much brain and not enough passion*

*I swear I could cure them.Here's Agamemnon, a nice enough
chap, and someone who loves the birds, but he's got more earwax
than brains; and that strange imitation of Jupiter there, his
brother, the bull, the model of all cuckolds, a useful but cheap tool,
a shoehorn hanging by a chain from Agamemnon's leg - to make him
look different, what should I do, spreading malice on my wit,
and stuffing wit with malice? To turn him into an ass would be nothing:
he is an ass and an ox. To turn him into an ox would be nothing: he is
 an ox and an ass.If I wasa dog, a mule, a cat, a polecat, a toad, a
lizard, an owl, a kite, or a barren herring, I would
not care; but if I had to be Menelaus, I would do anything to change
my fate. Don't ask me what I would be, if I wasn't Thersites; I wouldn't
want to be a leper's louse, so I wouldn't want to be Menelaus. Hello!
Fairies with fires!*

Enter HECTOR, TROILUS, AJAX, AGAMEMNON, ULYSSES,
NESTOR, MENELAUS, and DIOMEDES, with lights

AGAMEMNON.
We go wrong, we go wrong.

*I'm sure we've gone the wrong way.*

AJAX.
No, yonder 'tis;
There, where we see the lights.

*No, it's over there;
there, where you can see the light.*

HECTOR.
I trouble you.

*I'm giving you trouble.*

AJAX.
No, not a whit.

*No, not at all.*

Re-enter ACHILLES

ULYSSES.
Here comes himself to guide you.

*Here he comes himself to guide you.*

ACHILLES.
Welcome, brave Hector; welcome, Princes all.

*Welcome, brave Hector; welcome, all you princes.*

AGAMEMNON.
So now, fair Prince of Troy, I bid good night;
Ajax commands the guard to tend on you.

*So now, fair Prince of Troy, I'll say good night;*
*Ajax has been assigned to look after you.*

HECTOR.
Thanks, and good night to the Greeks' general.

*Thank you, and good night to the general of the Greeks.*

MENELAUS.
Good night, my lord.

*Good night, my lord.*

HECTOR.
Good night, sweet Lord Menelaus.

*Good night, sweet Lord Menelaus.*

THERSITES.
Sweet draught! 'Sweet' quoth 'a?
Sweet sink, sweet sewer!

*A sweetcesspool! 'Sweet' he says?*
*Sweet toilet, sweet sewer!*

ACHILLES.
Good night and welcome, both at once, to those
That go or tarry.

*Good night and welcome, both at the same time, to those*
*who are going and those who are staying.*

AGAMEMNON.
Good night.

*Good night.*

Exeunt AGAMEMNON and MENELAUS

ACHILLES.
Old Nestor tarries; and you too, Diomed,
Keep Hector company an hour or two.

*Old Nestor is staying; and you, Diomedes,*
*keep Hector company for an hour or two.*

DIOMEDES.
I cannot, lord; I have important business,
The tide whereof is now. Good night, great Hector.

*I cannot, Lord; I have important business,*
*which must be dealt with now. Good night, great Hector.*

HECTOR.
Give me your hand.

*Give me your hand.*

ULYSSES.
[Aside to TROILUS] Follow his torch; he goes to
Calchas' tent; I'll keep you company.

*Follow his torch; he's going to*
*Calchas' tent; I'll keep you company.*

TROILUS.
Sweet sir, you honour me.

*Sweet sir, you honour me.*

HECTOR.
And so, good night.

*And so, good night.*

Exit DIOMEDES; ULYSSES and TROILUS following

ACHILLES.
Come, come, enter my tent.

*Come on, come into my tent.*

Exeunt all but THERSITES

THERSITES.
That same Diomed's a false-hearted rogue, a most unjust
knave; I will no more trust him when he leers than I will a
serpent when he hisses. He will spend his mouth and promise, like
Brabbler the hound; but when he performs, astronomers foretell
it: it is prodigious, there will come some change; the sun
borrows of the moon when Diomed keeps his word. I will rather
leave to see Hector than not to dog him. They say he keeps a
Troyan drab, and uses the traitor Calchas' tent. I'll after.
Nothing but lechery! All incontinent varlets!
Exit

*That Diomedes is a false hearted scoundrel, a most dishonest
knave; I wouldn't trust him when he smiles any more than I trust
a snake when he hisses. He gives plenty of promises, like a
dog that's always barking; but when he actually makes good on them,
astrologers know it's going to happen: it's amazing, there must be a big change;
the sun gets light from the moon when Diomedes keeps his word. I would rather
not see Hector than miss the chance to follow him.
They say he has a Trojan tart, and uses the traitor Calchas' tent. I'll follow.
Nothing but lechery! What a bunch of randy scoundrels!*

## SCENE 2. The Grecian camp. Before CALCHAS' tent

Enter DIOMEDES

DIOMEDES.
What, are you up here, ho? Speak.

*Hello, is there anyone about? Speak.*

CALCHAS.
[Within] Who calls?

*Who's calling?*

DIOMEDES.
Diomed. Calchas, I think. Where's your daughter?

*Diomedes. That's Calchas, isn't it. Where's your daughter?*

CALCHAS.
[Within] She comes to you.

*She's coming to you.*

Enter TROILUS and ULYSSES, at a distance; after them
THERSITES

ULYSSES.
Stand where the torch may not discover us.

*Stand where they can't see the torch.*

Enter CRESSIDA

TROILUS.
Cressid comes forth to him.

*Cressida'scome out to him.*

DIOMEDES.

How now, my charge!

*Hello there, my charge!*

CRESSIDA.
Now, my sweet guardian! Hark, a word with you.
[Whispers]

*Hello, my sweet guardian! Listen, a word with you.*

TROILUS.
Yea, so familiar!

*Look, so familiar!*

ULYSSES.
She will sing any man at first sight.

*She attracts any man who sees her.*

THERSITES.
And any man may sing her, if he can take her clef;
she's noted.

*And any man can play with her, if he knows her key;
she is notorious for it.*

DIOMEDES.
Will you remember?

*Will you remember?*

CRESSIDA.
Remember? Yes.

*Remember? Yes.*

DIOMEDES.
Nay, but do, then;
And let your mind be coupled with your words.

*Well, make sure you do then;
and do as you said.*

TROILUS.
What shall she remember?

*What's he referring to?*

ULYSSES.
List!

*Listen!*

CRESSIDA.
Sweet honey Greek, tempt me no more to folly.

*You sweet as honey Greek, stop trying to tempt me to sin.*

THERSITES.
Roguery!

*Treachery!*

DIOMEDES.
Nay, then-

*No, then–*

CRESSIDA.
I'll tell you what-

*I'll tell you what–*

DIOMEDES.
Fo, fo! come, tell a pin; you are a forsworn-

*Enough! Don't trifle with me; you have promised–*

CRESSIDA.
In faith, I cannot. What would you have me do?

*I swear, I can't. What you want me to do?*

THERSITES.
A juggling trick, to be secretly open.

*A juggling trick, being a tart while seeming modest.*

DIOMEDES.
What did you swear you would bestow on me?

*What did you swear you would give me?*

CRESSIDA.
I prithee, do not hold me to mine oath;
Bid me do anything but that, sweet Greek.

*Please, don't hold me to my oath;*
*tell me to do anything but that, sweet Greek.*

DIOMEDES.
Good night.

*Good night.*

TROILUS.
Hold, patience!

*Stop there!*

ULYSSES.
How now, Troyan!

*What's this, Trojan!*

CRESSIDA.
Diomed!

*Diomedes!*

DIOMEDES.
No, no, good night; I'll be your fool no more.

*No, no, good night; I won't be your fool any more.*

TROILUS.
Thy better must.

*I expect better men will.*

CRESSIDA.

Hark! a word in your ear.

*Listen! Let me have a word.*

TROILUS.
O plague and madness!

*Oh plague and madness!*

ULYSSES.
You are moved, Prince; let us depart, I pray,
Lest your displeasure should enlarge itself
To wrathful terms. This place is dangerous;
The time right deadly; I beseech you, go.

*You are upset, Prince; let's go, please,
in case your displeasure should lead
to anopen quarrel. This place is dangerous;
it's a perilous time; I beg you, go.*

TROILUS.
Behold, I pray you.

*Watch, please.*

ULYSSES.
Nay, good my lord, go off;
You flow to great distraction; come, my lord.

*No, my good lord, let's go;
this is making you mad; come on, my lord.*

TROILUS.
I prithee stay.

*I ask you to stay.*

ULYSSES.
You have not patience; come.

*You won't be able to control yourself; come on.*

TROILUS.
I pray you, stay; by hell and all hell's torments,

I will not speak a word.

*Please, stay; I swear by hell and all its tortures,*
*I won't say a word.*

DIOMEDES.
And so, good night.

*And so, good night.*

CRESSIDA.
Nay, but you part in anger.

*No, but you're leaving angry.*

TROILUS.
Doth that grieve thee? O withered truth!

*Does that upset you? How your honesty has gone!*

ULYSSES.
How now, my lord?

*What's this, my lord?*

TROILUS.
By Jove, I will be patient.

*I swear, I will be calm.*

CRESSIDA.
Guardian! Why, Greek!

*Guardian! Why, Greek!*

DIOMEDES.
Fo, fo! adieu! you palter.

*Whatever! Goodbye! You're messing me around.*

CRESSIDA.
In faith, I do not. Come hither once again.

*I swear, I'm not. Please come back here.*

ULYSSES.
You shake, my lord, at something; will you go?
You will break out.

*You're shaking, my lord, at something; will you go?*
*You will explode.*

TROILUS.
She strokes his cheek.

*She's stroking his cheek.*

ULYSSES.
Come, come.

*Come, come.*

TROILUS.
Nay, stay; by Jove, I will not speak a word:
There is between my will and all offences
A guard of patience. Stay a little while.

*No, stay; by Jove, I won't say a word:*
*my self-control will stop me following*
*my anger. Stay a little while.*

THERSITES.
How the devil luxury, with his fat rump and potato
finger, tickles these together! Fry, lechery, fry!

*How the devil lechery, with his fat behind and*
*tickling fingers, winds these people up! Burn, lechery, burn!*

DIOMEDES.
But will you, then?

*So will you do it?*

CRESSIDA.
In faith, I will, lo; never trust me else.

*I promise I will; otherwise never trust me.*

DIOMEDES.
Give me some token for the surety of it.

*Give me some token to prove it.*

CRESSIDA.
I'll fetch you one.

*I'll get one for you.*

Exit

ULYSSES.
You have sworn patience.

*You have sworn to be calm.*

TROILUS.
Fear me not, my lord;
I will not be myself, nor have cognition
Of what I feel. I am all patience.

*Don't worry about me, my lord;*
*I won't be myself, or acknowledge*
*my feelings. I am all calm.*

Re-enter CRESSIDA

THERSITES.
Now the pledge; now, now, now!

*Now the promise; now, now, now!*

CRESSIDA.
Here, Diomed, keep this sleeve.

*Here, Diomedes, keep this cuff.*

TROILUS.
O beauty! where is thy faith?

*O beauty! Where is your loyalty?*

ULYSSES.

My lord!

*My Lord!*

TROILUS.
I will be patient; outwardly I will.

*I will be calm; on the outside I will.*

CRESSIDA.
You look upon that sleeve; behold it well.
He lov'd me-O false wench!-Give't me again.

*You're looking at that cuff; examine it well.*
*He loved me–you false girl!–Give it back to me.*

DIOMEDES.
Whose was't?

*Who's was it?*

CRESSIDA.
It is no matter, now I ha't again.
I will not meet with you to-morrow night.
I prithee, Diomed, visit me no more.

*It doesn't matter, now I have it back.*
*I won't meet you tomorrow night.*
*Please, Diomedes, never visit me again.*

THERSITES.
Now she sharpens. Well said, whetstone.

*Now she's getting sharper. Well said, sharpener.*

DIOMEDES.
I shall have it.

*I shall have it.*

CRESSIDA.
What, this?

*What, this?*

DIOMEDES.
Ay, that.

*Yes, that.*

CRESSIDA.
O all you gods! O pretty, pretty pledge!
Thy master now lies thinking on his bed
Of thee and me, and sighs, and takes my glove,
And gives memorial dainty kisses to it,
As I kiss thee. Nay, do not snatch it from me;
He that takes that doth take my heart withal.

*Oh all you gods! Oh this pretty token!*
*Your master is now lying on his bed thinking*
*about you and me, and is sighing, taking my glove,*
*and giving little kisses of remembrance to it,*
*as I kiss you. No, do not snatch it from me;*
*if you take that you take my heart as well.*

DIOMEDES.
I had your heart before; this follows it.

*I had your heart before; this goes with it.*

TROILUS.
I did swear patience.

*I swore to be calm.*

CRESSIDA.
You shall not have it, Diomed; faith, you shall not;
I'll give you something else.

*You shall not have it, Diomedes; I swear, you shall not;*
*I'll give you something else.*

DIOMEDES.
I will have this. Whose was it?

*I want this. Whose was it?*

CRESSIDA.

226

It is no matter.

*It's not important.*

DIOMEDES.
Come, tell me whose it was.

*Come, tell me who's it was.*

CRESSIDA.
'Twas one's that lov'd me better than you will.
But, now you have it, take it.

*It belonged to someone who loved me better than you will.*
*But, now you have it, take it.*

DIOMEDES.
Whose was it?

*Whose was it?*

CRESSIDA.
By all Diana's waiting women yond,
And by herself, I will not tell you whose.

*By all Diana's attendant stars up there,*
*and by herself, I swear I will not tell you.*

DIOMEDES.
To-morrow will I wear it on my helm,
And grieve his spirit that dares not challenge it.

*Tomorrow I will wear it on my helmet,*
*and torture the soul of someone who dares not challenge it.*

TROILUS.
Wert thou the devil and wor'st it on thy horn,
It should be challeng'd.

*If you were the devil andwore it on your horns,*
*you would be challenged.*

CRESSIDA.
Well, well, 'tis done, 'tis past; and yet it is not;

I will not keep my word.

*Well, well, it's finished, it's over; but it isn't;*
*I won't keep my word.*

DIOMEDES.
Why, then farewell;
Thou never shalt mock Diomed again.

*Well then, goodbye;*
*you will never mock Diomedes again.*

CRESSIDA.
You shall not go. One cannot speak a word
But it straight starts you.

*You shan't go. One can't say anything*
*without setting you off.*

DIOMEDES.
I do not like this fooling.

*I don't like this fooling about.*

THERSITES.
Nor I, by Pluto; but that that likes not you
Pleases me best.

*Nor do I, by Pluto; but what you don't like*
*I like the most.*

DIOMEDES.
What, shall I come? The hour-

*What, shall I come? The time–*

CRESSIDA.
Ay, come-O Jove! Do come. I shall be plagu'd.

*Yes, come–oh Jove! Do come. What a life I have!*

DIOMEDES.
Farewell till then.

———

228

*Farewell until then.*

CRESSIDA.
Good night. I prithee come. Exit DIOMEDES
Troilus, farewell! One eye yet looks on thee;
But with my heart the other eye doth see.
Ah, poor our sex! this fault in us I find,
The error of our eye directs our mind.
What error leads must err; O, then conclude,
Minds sway'd by eyes are full of turpitude.
Exit

*Good night. Please come.*
*Troilus, farewell! One of my eyes still looks at you;*
*but my heart is seeing with the other.*
*Ah, how poor women are! I find this fault in us,*
*that our wandering eyes direct our minds.*
*When you wander from the path you must make mistakes; so we see*
*that minds governed by eyes are depraved.*

THERSITES.
A proof of strength she could not publish more,
Unless she said 'My mind is now turn'd whore.'

*She couldn't give clearer evidence,*
*unless she said, 'I have now become a whore.'*

ULYSSES.
All's done, my lord.

*It's over, my lord.*

TROILUS.
It is.

*It is.*

ULYSSES.
Why stay we, then?

*Why are we staying, then?*

TROILUS.
To make a recordation to my soul

Of every syllable that here was spoke.
But if I tell how these two did coact,
Shall I not lie in publishing a truth?
Sith yet there is a credence in my heart,
An esperance so obstinately strong,
That doth invert th' attest of eyes and ears;
As if those organs had deceptious functions
Created only to calumniate.
Was Cressid here?

*To make sure I clearly remember*
*every syllable that was spoken here.*
*But if I tell how these two carried on together,*
*won't I be lying when publishing the truth?*
*Since there is still a belief in my heart,*
*a hope so obstinately strong,*
*that it rejects the proof of eyes and ears,*
*as if those organs were deceivers,*
*created only to slander.*
*Was Cressida here?*

ULYSSES.
I cannot conjure, Troyan.

*I'm not a magician, Trojan, I couldn't have conjured her up.*

TROILUS.
She was not, sure.

*I'm sure she wasn't.*

ULYSSES.
Most sure she was.

*She definitely was.*

TROILUS.
Why, my negation hath no taste of madness.

*My denial of this is not madness.*

ULYSSES.
Nor mine, my lord. Cressid was here but now.

*Nor is what I say, my lord. Cressida was here just now.*

TROILUS.
Let it not be believ'd for womanhood.
Think, we had mothers; do not give advantage
To stubborn critics, apt, without a theme,
For depravation, to square the general sex
By Cressid's rule. Rather think this not Cressid.

*Let no one believe that, for the sake of womanhood!*
*Think, we had mothers. Don't give ammunition*
*to harsh critics, who will, when they don't have*
*specific grounds to accuse women, will say they are all*
*like Cressida. Better to think that this wasn't Cressida.*

ULYSSES.
What hath she done, Prince, that can soil our mothers?

*What has she done, Prince, that can stain our mothers?*

TROILUS.
Nothing at all, unless that this were she.

*Nothing at all, unless this was her.*

THERSITES.
Will 'a swagger himself out on's own eyes?

*Is he going to talk himself out of believing the evidence of his own eyes?*

TROILUS.
This she? No; this is Diomed's Cressida.
If beauty have a soul, this is not she;
If souls guide vows, if vows be sanctimonies,
If sanctimony be the god's delight,
If there be rule in unity itself,
This was not she. O madness of discourse,
That cause sets up with and against itself!
Bifold authority! where reason can revolt
Without perdition, and loss assume all reason
Without revolt: this is, and is not, Cressid.
Within my soul there doth conduce a fight
Of this strange nature, that a thing inseparate
Divides more wider than the sky and earth;

And yet the spacious breadth of this division
Admits no orifex for a point as subtle
As Ariachne's broken woof to enter.
Instance, O instance! strong as Pluto's gates:
Cressid is mine, tied with the bonds of heaven.
Instance, O instance! strong as heaven itself:
The bonds of heaven are slipp'd, dissolv'd, and loos'd;
And with another knot, five-finger-tied,
The fractions of her faith, orts of her love,
The fragments, scraps, the bits, and greasy relics
Of her o'er-eaten faith, are bound to Diomed.

*This one? No, this is Diomedes' Cressida.*
*If beauty has a soul, this is not her;*
*if souls keep vows, if vows are holy,*
*if holiness delights the gods,*
*if things can only be one thing,*
*this was not her. What a mad argument,*
*that sets up arguments for and against itself!*
*A complete contradiction, when reasoning can*
*contradict itself without damaging itself,*
*and when unreasonableness can seem rational*
*without contradiction! This is and is not Cressida.*
*There is a fight going on within my soul*
*of a strange type, thinking that an indivisible thing*
*has been divided wider than the sky and earth,*
*and yet the great gap this has created*
*hasn't given the space big enough for something as small*
*as a spider's web to go through it.*
*As an example, as strong as the gates of hell,*
*Cressida is mine, tied to me with heavenly bonds;*
*as an example, as strong as heaven itself,*
*the bonds of heaven have been thrown off,*
*and another knot, impossible to untie,*
*has bound the fragments of her faith, the leftovers of her love,*
*all the filthy greasy scraps of the meal of her*
*finished fidelity, to Diomedes.*

ULYSSES.
May worthy Troilus be half-attach'd
With that which here his passion doth express?

*Is worthy Troilus half as much moved*
*as he appears to be?*

TROILUS.
Ay, Greek; and that shall be divulged well
In characters as red as Mars his heart
Inflam'd with Venus. Never did young man fancy
With so eternal and so fix'd a soul.
Hark, Greek: as much as I do Cressid love,
So much by weight hate I her Diomed.
That sleeve is mine that he'll bear on his helm;
Were it a casque compos'd by Vulcan's skill
My sword should bite it. Not the dreadful spout
Which shipmen do the hurricano call,
Constring'd in mass by the almighty sun,
Shall dizzy with more clamour Neptune's ear
In his descent than shall my prompted sword
Falling on Diomed.

*Yes, Greek; and I'll show my passion*
*with actions as bloody as the heart of Mars*
*inflamed with Venus. No young man ever loved*
*with such constancy and fidelity.*
*Listen, Greek: the amount that I love Cressida,*
*that's the same amount I hate Diomedes.*
*He will wear my cuff on his helmet;*
*if that was a headpiece made by Vulcan*
*my sword would still cut into it. The dreadful waterspout*
*which sailors call a hurricane,*
*with its weight compressed by the almighty sun,*
*won't make more noise as it tears up the sea*
*than my sword will when it falls on Diomedes.*

THERSITES.
He'll tickle it for his concupy.

*He'lltickle it in revenge for his whore.*

TROILUS.
O Cressid! O false Cressid! false, false, false!
Let all untruths stand by thy stained name,
And they'll seem glorious.

*O Cressida! Oh false Cressida! False, false, false!*
*Let all lies stand next to your stained name,*
*it will make them seem wonderful.*

ULYSSES.
O, contain yourself;
Your passion draws ears hither.

*O, control yourself;*
*your passion is attracting attention.*

Enter AENEAS

AENEAS.
I have been seeking you this hour, my lord.
Hector, by this, is arming him in Troy;
Ajax, your guard, stays to conduct you home.

*I have been looking for you for an hour, my lord.*
*By this time Hector is arming himself in Troy.*
*Ajax, your guard, is waiting to escort you home.*

TROILUS.
Have with you, Prince. My courteous lord, adieu.
Fairwell, revolted fair!-and, Diomed,
Stand fast and wear a castle on thy head.

*I'm coming, Prince. My sweet lord, goodbye.*
*Farewell, faceless beauty! And, Diomedes,*
*get ready and wear a strong helmet.*

ULYSSES.
I'll bring you to the gates.

*I'll come with you to the gates.*

TROILUS.
Accept distracted thanks.

*I give you my thanks, though my mind is elsewhere.*

Exeunt TROILUS, AENEAS. and ULYSSES

THERSITES.
Would I could meet that rogue Diomed! I would croak like
a raven; I would bode, I would bode. Patroclus will give me
anything for the intelligence of this whore; the parrot will not

do more for an almond than he for a commodious drab. Lechery, lechery! Still wars and lechery! Nothing else holds fashion. A burning devil take them!
Exit

*I wish I could fight that rogue Diomedes! I would croak like a raven, I would foretell disaster. Patroclus will give me anything I want for information about this whore; he'll do as much to get a willing tart as a parrot will for an almond. Lechery, lechery! Still wars and lechery! Nothing else is in fashion. May the devil take them off to hell!*

# SCENE 3. Troy. Before PRIAM'S palace

Enter HECTOR and ANDROMACHE

ANDROMACHE.
When was my lord so much ungently temper'd
To stop his ears against admonishment?
Unarm, unarm, and do not fight to-day.

*Since when has my lord become so impolite*
*now he won't listen to advice?*
*Take your armour off, and do not fight today.*

HECTOR.
You train me to offend you; get you in.
By all the everlasting gods, I'll go.

*You're asking me to offend you; go inside.*
*By all the eternal gods, I'll go.*

ANDROMACHE.
My dreams will, sure, prove ominous to the day.

*I'm sure my dreams will prove prophetic about this day.*

HECTOR.
No more, I say.

*I'm telling you, no more.*

Enter CASSANDRA

CASSANDRA.
Where is my brother Hector?

*Where is my brother Hector?*

ANDROMACHE.
Here, sister, arm'd, and bloody in intent.
Consort with me in loud and dear petition,

Pursue we him on knees; for I have dreamt
Of bloody turbulence, and this whole night
Hath nothing been but shapes and forms of slaughter.

*Here, sister, armed, and with bloody intentions.*
*Join me in a loud and passionate petition;*
*let's follow him on our knees; for I have dreamt*
*of bloody disturbances, and all night long*
*I have seen nothing but visions of slaughter.*

CASSANDRA.
O, 'tis true!

*Oh, it's true!*

HECTOR.
Ho! bid my trumpet sound.

*Ho! Tell them to blow my trumpet.*

CASSANDRA.
No notes of sally, for the heavens, sweet brother!

*No orders to attack, for heaven's sake, sweet brother!*

HECTOR.
Be gone, I say. The gods have heard me swear.

*I'm telling you, go away. I have sworn to the gods.*

CASSANDRA.
The gods are deaf to hot and peevish vows;
They are polluted off'rings, more abhorr'd
Than spotted livers in the sacrifice.

*The gods don't listen to angry and foolish vows;*
*they are polluted offerings, more hated*
*than offering diseased animals for sacrifice.*

ANDROMACHE.
O, be persuaded! Do not count it holy
To hurt by being just. It is as lawful,
For we would give much, to use violent thefts
And rob in the behalf of charity.

*Oh, listen to her! Don't think that it's holy*
*to cause hurt by sticking to a vow. It would be just as lawful*
*to commit violent thefts just because*
*we wanted to give lots of charity.*

CASSANDRA.
It is the purpose that makes strong the vow;
But vows to every purpose must not hold.
Unarm, sweet Hector.

*The reason for the vow is what makes it sacred;*
*but not every reason makes every vow sacred.*
*Disarm, sweet Hector.*

HECTOR.
Hold you still, I say.
Mine honour keeps the weather of my fate.
Life every man holds dear; but the dear man
Holds honour far more precious dear than life.
Enter TROILUS
How now, young man! Mean'st thou to fight to-day?

*Keep quiet, I say.*
*My honour is superior to my life.*
*Every man thinks life is good; but the good man*
*think honour is far more good than life.*

*Hello there, young man! Do you mean to fight today?*

ANDROMACHE.
Cassandra, call my father to persuade.

*Cassandra, call my father to reason with him.*

Exit CASSANDRA

HECTOR.
No, faith, young Troilus; doff thy harness, youth;
I am to-day i' th' vein of chivalry.
Let grow thy sinews till their knots be strong,
And tempt not yet the brushes of the war.
Unarm thee, go; and doubt thou not, brave boy,
I'll stand to-day for thee and me and Troy.

*No, indeed, young Troilus; take off your armour, young man;*
*today I am in the mood for knightly deeds.*
*Let your muscles grow until they are stronger,*
*and don't yet attempt the dangers of war.*
*Disarm yourself, go; and do not doubt, brave boy,*
*today I will represent you and me and Troy.*

TROILUS.
Brother, you have a vice of mercy in you
Which better fits a lion than a man.

*Brother, you have a weakness of mercy in you*
*which is more suited to a lion than a man.*

HECTOR.
What vice is that, good Troilus?
Chide me for it.

*What weaknesses is that, good Troilus?*
*Tell me off for it.*

TROILUS.
When many times the captive Grecian falls,
Even in the fan and wind of your fair sword,
You bid them rise and live.

*Often when the miserable Greek falls,*
*right within the reach of your great sword,*
*you tell them to get up and live.*

HECTOR.
O, 'tis fair play!

*Oh, that's fair play!*

TROILUS.
Fool's play, by heaven, Hector.

*Fool's play, I swear, Hector.*

HECTOR.
How now! how now!

*What! What!*

TROILUS.
For th' love of all the gods,
Let's leave the hermit Pity with our mother;
And when we have our armours buckled on,
The venom'd vengeance ride upon our swords,
Spur them to ruthful work, rein them from ruth!

*For the love of all gods,*
*let's leave the holy pity at home with our mother;*
*and when we have strapped on our armour,*
*let poisonous vengeance drive our swords onwards*
*to terrible work, don't let them show pity!*

HECTOR.
Fie, savage, fie!

*Enough, savage, enough!*

TROILUS.
Hector, then 'tis wars.

*Hector, this is war.*

HECTOR.
Troilus, I would not have you fight to-day.

*Troilus, I don't want you to fight today.*

TROILUS.
Who should withhold me?
Not fate, obedience, nor the hand of Mars
Beck'ning with fiery truncheon my retire;
Not Priamus and Hecuba on knees,
Their eyes o'ergalled with recourse of tears;
Nor you, my brother, with your true sword drawn,
Oppos'd to hinder me, should stop my way,
But by my ruin.

*Who's going to stop me?*
*Not fate, obedience, nor the hand of Mars*
*ordering me to retreat with his fiery staff;*
*not Priam or Hecuba on their knees,*

*their eyes sore with tears;*
*nor you, my brother, with your true sword drawn,*
*poised to stop me, will block my way,*
*except by killing me.*

Re-enter CASSANDRA, with PRIAM

CASSANDRA.
Lay hold upon him, Priam, hold him fast;
He is thy crutch; now if thou lose thy stay,
Thou on him leaning, and all Troy on thee,
Fall all together.

*Get hold of him, Priam, hold him fast;*
*he is your crutch; now if you let go of your support,*
*leaning on him, with all Troy leaning on you,*
*you will all fall down together.*

PRIAM.
Come, Hector, come, go back.
Thy wife hath dreamt; thy mother hath had visions;
Cassandra doth foresee; and I myself
Am like a prophet suddenly enrapt
To tell thee that this day is ominous.
Therefore, come back.

*Come, Hector, go back.*
*Your wife has dreamt, your mother has had visions,*
*Cassandra has predicted, and I myself*
*am like a prophet suddenly overcome with foresight,*
*telling you that this day is dangerous.*
*So, come back inside.*

HECTOR.
Aeneas is a-field;
And I do stand engag'd to many Greeks,
Even in the faith of valour, to appear
This morning to them.

*Aeneas is on the battlefield;*
*and I have a commitment to many Greeks,*
*having pledged my valour, to appear*
*to them this morning.*

PRIAM.
Ay, but thou shalt not go.

*Yes, but you shan't go.*

HECTOR.
I must not break my faith.
You know me dutiful; therefore, dear sir,
Let me not shame respect; but give me leave
To take that course by your consent and voice
Which you do here forbid me, royal Priam.

*I must not break my promise.*
*You know that I am obedient; therefore, dear sir,*
*don't make me disrespect you; give me permission*
*with your agreement and words to do the thing*
*which you are forbidding me, royal Priam.*

CASSANDRA.
O Priam, yield not to him!

*O Priam, don't give in to him!*

ANDROMACHE.
Do not, dear father.

*Do not, dear father.*

HECTOR.
Andromache, I am offended with you.
Upon the love you bear me, get you in.

*Andromache, I'm angry with you.*
*By the love you have for me, go inside.*

Exit ANDROMACHE

TROILUS.
This foolish, dreaming, superstitious girl
Makes all these bodements.

*This foolish, dreaming, superstitious girl*
*makes all these predictions.*

242

CASSANDRA.
O, farewell, dear Hector!
Look how thou diest. Look how thy eye turns pale.
Look how thy wounds do bleed at many vents.
Hark how Troy roars; how Hecuba cries out;
How poor Andromache shrills her dolours forth;
Behold distraction, frenzy, and amazement,
Like witless antics, one another meet,
And all cry, Hector! Hector's dead! O Hector!

*Oh, farewell, dear Hector!*
*Look how you're dying. Look how your eye turns pale.*
*Look how your wounds bleed from many cuts.*
*Hear how Troy is roaring; how Hecuba is crying;*
*how poor Andromache screams out her sorrows;*
*see how madness, frenzy and bewilderment*
*meet each other like witless clowns,*
*and all are crying, 'Hector! Hector is dead! Oh, Hector!'*

TROILUS.
Away, away!

*Go away!*

CASSANDRA.
Farewell!-yet, soft! Hector, I take my leave.
Thou dost thyself and all our Troy deceive.
Exit

*Farewell! But, a moment! Hector, I am going.*
*You are deceiving yourself and betraying all of Troy.*

HECTOR.
You are amaz'd, my liege, at her exclaim.
Go in, and cheer the town; we'll forth, and fight,
Do deeds worth praise and tell you them at night.

*You are perplexed, my lord, at her outburst.*
*Go inside, and rally the town; we'll go out, and fight,*
*do praiseworthy deeds and we'll tell you about them at night.*

PRIAM.
Farewell. The gods with safety stand about thee!

*Farewell. May the gods protect you!*

Exeunt severally PRIAM and HECTOR.

Alarums

TROILUS.
They are at it, hark! Proud Diomed, believe,
I come to lose my arm or win my sleeve.

*They have begun, listen! Proud Diomedes, believe me,*
*I shall lose my arm or win back my cuff.*

Enter PANDARUS

PANDARUS.
Do you hear, my lord? Do you hear?

*Have you heard, my lord? Have you heard?*

TROILUS.
What now?

*What now?*

PANDARUS.
Here's a letter come from yond poor girl.

*Here's a letter come from the poor girl out there.*

TROILUS.
Let me read.

*Let me read it.*

PANDARUS.
A whoreson tisick, a whoreson rascally tisick so troubles
me, and the foolish fortune of this girl, and what one thing,
what another, that I shall leave you one o' th's days; and I have
a rheum in mine eyes too, and such an ache in my bones that
unless a man were curs'd I cannot tell what to think on't. What
says she there?

*A bitching cough, a bitching rascally cough is giving me*

244

so much trouble, along with the unlucky fortunes of this girl, what with one thing
and another I shall be leaving you one of these days; and I have
water in my eyes too, and such an ache in my bones that
unless I was suffering from a curse I don't know what could have caused it.
What does she say there?

TROILUS.
Words, words, mere words, no matter from the heart;
Th' effect doth operate another way.
[Tearing the letter]
Go, wind, to wind! Here turn and change together.
My love with words and errors still she feeds,
But edifies another with her deeds. Exeunt severally

*Words, words, just words, nothing heartfelt;*
*things are quite different in practice.*
*[Tearing the letter]*
*Empty words into the air! There you can mix up as you please.*
*She is still feeding my love with words and deceit,*
*but in practice she's with someone else.*

# SCENE 4. The plain between Troy and the Grecian camp

Enter THERSITES. Excursions

THERSITES.
Now they are clapper-clawing one another; I'll go look on. That dissembling abominable varlet, Diomed, has got that same scurvy doting foolish young knave's sleeve of Troy there in his helm. I would fain see them meet, that that same young Troyan ass that loves the whore there might send that Greekish whoremasterly villain with the sleeve back to the dissembling luxurious drab of a sleeve-less errand. A th' t'other side, the policy of those crafty swearing rascals-that stale old mouse-eaten dry cheese, Nestor, and that same dog-fox, Ulysses -is not prov'd worth a blackberry. They set me up, in policy, that mongrel cur, Ajax, against that dog of as bad a kind, Achilles; and now is the cur, Ajax prouder than the cur Achilles, and will not arm to-day; whereupon the Grecians begin to proclaim barbarism, and policy grows into an ill opinion.
Enter DIOMEDES, TROILUS following
Soft! here comes sleeve, and t'other.

*Now they are bashing away at each other;*
*I'll go and watch. That horrible deceitful scoundrel,*
*Diomedes, has the cuff of that foolish indulgent stupid*
*young knave of Troy in his helmet. I would love to see*
*them meet, and see that same young Trojan ass that loves*
*that whore send that pimping Greek villain*
*who has the sleeve back to his lying lecherous*
*whore without it. On the other side, the cunning plan*
*of those crafty swearing rascals—that stale old mouse*
*eaten dry cheese, Nestor, and that dog fox,*
*Ulysses—has been proved to be not worth a damn.*
*For their own crafty purposes they set that mongrel Ajax*
*against that equally bad dog, Achilles. And now the dog Ajax is prouder*
*than the dog Achilles, and won't go to battle today,*
*and because of this the Greeks begin to embrace barbarism,*
*and the plans are all falling apart.*

*Hush! Here comes the one with the cuff, and the other.*

TROILUS.
Fly not; for shouldst thou take the river Styx
I would swim after.

*Don't run; if you should jump into the river Styx*
*I would swim after you.*

DIOMEDES.
Thou dost miscall retire.
I do not fly; but advantageous care
Withdrew me from the odds of multitude.
Have at thee.

*You are misdescribing my tactical retreat.*
*I was not running; in order to get a better advantage*
*I drew back in the face of greater numbers.*
*Take that.*

THERSITES.
Hold thy whore, Grecian; now for thy whore,
Troyan-now the sleeve, now the sleeve!

*Fight for your whore, Greek; now for your whore,*
*Trojan–now for the cuff, the cuff!*

Exeunt TROILUS and DIOMEDES fighting

Enter HECTOR

HECTOR.
What art thou, Greek? Art thou for Hector's match?
Art thou of blood and honour?

*Who are you, Greek? Are you a match for Hector?*
*Do you have rank and honour?*

THERSITES.
No, no-I am a rascal; a scurvy railing knave; a very
filthy rogue.

*No, no–I am a rascal; a filthy whining knave; a very*
*dirty rogue.*

HECTOR.
I do believe thee. Live.
Exit

*I believe you. Live.*

THERSITES.
God-a-mercy, that thou wilt believe me; but a plague
break thy neck for frighting me! What's become of the wenching
rogues? I think they have swallowed one another. I would laugh at
that miracle. Yet, in a sort, lechery eats itself. I'll seek
them.
Exit

*Thank God, that you believed me; but I hope*
*you break your neck for frightening me! What's become of those lustful*
*rogues? I think they have swallowed each other up. I would laugh at*
*that miracle. But, in a way, lechery consumes itself. I'll look for them.*

## SCENE 5. Another part of the plain

Enter DIOMEDES and A SERVANT

DIOMEDES.
Go, go, my servant, take thou Troilus' horse;
Present the fair steed to my lady Cressid.
Fellow, commend my service to her beauty;
Tell her I have chastis'd the amorous Troyan,
And am her knight by proof.

*Go, go, my servant, take Troilus' horse;*
*give it to my lady Cressida.*
*Fellow, tell her I am the servant of her beauty;*
*tell her I have beaten the amorous Trojan,*
*and have proved that I am her knight.*

SERVANT.
I go, my lord.
Exit

*I'm going, my lord.*

Enter AGAMEMNON

AGAMEMNON.
Renew, renew! The fierce Polydamus
Hath beat down Menon; bastard Margarelon
Hath Doreus prisoner,
And stands colossus-wise, waving his beam,
Upon the pashed corses of the kings
Epistrophus and Cedius. Polixenes is slain;
Amphimacus and Thoas deadly hurt;
Patroclus ta'en, or slain; and Palamedes
Sore hurt and bruis'd. The dreadful Sagittary
Appals our numbers. Haste we, Diomed,
To reinforcement, or we perish all.

*Regroup, regroup! The fierce Polydamus*
*has beaten down Menon; bastard Margarelon*

*is holding Doreous prisoner;*
*and is standing like a colossus, waving his spear,*
*over the battered corpses of the Kings*
*Epistrophus and Cedius.Polixenes is slain;*
*Amphimacus and Thoas are mortally wounded;*
*Patroclus is captured or slain; and Palamedes*
*is desperately wounded.The dreadful Centaur*
*is terrifying our forces. Let's hurry, Diomedes,*
*to bring up reinforcements, or we shall all die.*

Enter NESTOR

NESTOR.
Go, bear Patroclus' body to Achilles,
And bid the snail-pac'd Ajax arm for shame.
There is a thousand Hectors in the field;
Now here he fights on Galathe his horse,
And there lacks work; anon he's there afoot,
And there they fly or die, like scaled sculls
Before the belching whale; then is he yonder,
And there the strawy Greeks, ripe for his edge,
Fall down before him like the mower's swath.
Here, there, and everywhere, he leaves and takes;
Dexterity so obeying appetite
That what he will he does, and does so much
That proof is call'd impossibility.

*Go, carry Patroclus' body to Achilles,*
*and tell the sluggardly Ajax to be ashamed and arm himself.*
*There seem to be a thousand Hectors on the field;*
*now here his fighting on Galathe his horse,*
*then doesn't have enough to do; so soon he's there on foot,*
*and their they flee or die like schools of fish*
*fleeing from a whale; then he's over there,*
*and there the Greeks are like grass, ready to be mown,*
*and they fall down before him like scythed wheat.*
*Here, there and everywhere he chops and slices,*
*his skill so matching his desire*
*that he does exactly what he wants, and what he does*
*seems almost impossible.*

Enter ULYSSES

ULYSSES.

O, courage, courage, courage, Princes! Great
Achilles Is arming, weeping, cursing, vowing vengeance.
Patroclus' wounds have rous'd his drowsy blood,
Together with his mangled Myrmidons,
That noseless, handless, hack'd and chipp'd, come to
him, Crying on Hector. Ajax hath lost a friend
And foams at mouth, and he is arm'd and at it,
Roaring for Troilus; who hath done to-day
Mad and fantastic execution,
Engaging and redeeming of himself
With such a careless force and forceless care
As if that luck, in very spite of cunning,
Bade him win all.

*Oh, courage, courage, courage, Princes! Great*
*Achilles is arming, weeping, cursing, vowing vengeance.*
*Patroclus' wounds have awoken his lazy passion,*
*together with his bastard Myrmidons,*
*who, noseless, handless, hacked and chopped, come to*
*him, crying out against Hector. Ajax has lost a friend*
*and foams at the mouth, and he is armed and fighting,*
*roaring for Troilus; he today has committed*
*incredible angry slaughter,*
*throwing himself in and then freeing himself*
*with such cool use of strength and effortless defence*
*it seemed that luck, in spite of the skill of his enemies,*
*had told him he would win everything.*

Enter AJAX

AJAX.
Troilus! thou coward Troilus!
Exit

*Troilus! You coward Troilus!*

DIOMEDES.
Ay, there, there.

*Yes, there, there.*

NESTOR.
So, so, we draw together.
Exit

*So, so, we all come together.*

Enter ACHILLES

ACHILLES.
Where is this Hector?
Come, come, thou boy-queller, show thy face;
Know what it is to meet Achilles angry.
Hector! where's Hector? I will none but Hector.
Exeunt

*Where is this Hector?*
*Come, come, you child killer, show your face;*
*learn what it is to fight Achilles when he is angry.*
*Hector! Where's Hector? I will fight nobody but Hector.*

# SCENE 6. Another part of the plain

Enter AJAX

AJAX.
Troilus, thou coward Troilus, show thy head.

*Troilus, you coward Troilus, show your face.*

Enter DIOMEDES

DIOMEDES.
Troilus, I say! Where's Troilus?

*Troilus, I say! Where's Troilus?*

AJAX.
What wouldst thou?

*What do you want?*

DIOMEDES.
I would correct him.

*I want to punish him.*

AJAX.
Were I the general, thou shouldst have my office
Ere that correction. Troilus, I say! What, Troilus!

*If I were the general, I would give you my job*
*rather than let you have that pleasure. Troilus, I say! What, Troilus!*

Enter TROILUS

TROILUS.
O traitor Diomed! Turn thy false face, thou traitor,
And pay thy life thou owest me for my horse.

*Oh you traitor Diomedes! Turn and face me, you traitor,*

*and pay the life you owe me for my horse.*

DIOMEDES.
Ha! art thou there?

*Ha! Is that you?*

AJAX.
I'll fight with him alone. Stand, Diomed.

*I'll fight him single-handed. Stand aside, Diomedes.*

DIOMEDES.
He is my prize. I will not look upon.

*He's my prize. I won't stand by and watch.*

TROILUS.
Come, both, you cogging Greeks; have at you!

*Come on, both of you, you deceitful Greeks. Take that!*

Exeunt fighting

Enter HECTOR

HECTOR.
Yea, Troilus? O, well fought, my youngest brother!

*Is that Troilus? Oh, well fought, my youngest brother!*

Enter ACHILLES

ACHILLES.
Now do I see thee, ha! Have at thee, Hector!

*Now I see you! Take that, Hector!*

HECTOR.
Pause, if thou wilt.

*Wait, if you will.*

ACHILLES.

I do disdain thy courtesy, proud Troyan.
Be happy that my arms are out of use;
My rest and negligence befriends thee now,
But thou anon shalt hear of me again;
Till when, go seek thy fortune.
Exit

*I refuse you politeness, arrogant Trojan.*
*Be glad that I'm out of training;*
*my rest and laziness is in your favour,*
*but soon you will hear from me again;*
*until then, good luck.*

HECTOR.
Fare thee well.
I would have been much more a fresher man,
Had I expected thee.

*Farewell.*
*I would have kept myself fresher,*
*if I'd known you were coming.*

Re-enter TROILUS

How now, my brother!

*Hello, my brother!*

TROILUS.
Ajax hath ta'en Aeneas. Shall it be?
No, by the flame of yonder glorious heaven,
He shall not carry him; I'll be ta'en too,
Or bring him off. Fate, hear me what I say:
I reck not though thou end my life to-day.
Exit

*Ajax has captured Aeneas.Shall this happen?*
*No, I swear by the sun,*
*he shan't take him, either I'll be captured too*
*or I'll rescue him.Fate, hear what I say;*
*I don't care if you take my life today.*

Enter one in armour

HECTOR.
Stand, stand, thou Greek; thou art a goodly mark.
No? wilt thou not? I like thy armour well;
I'll frush it and unlock the rivets all
But I'll be master of it. Wilt thou not, beast, abide?
Why then, fly on; I'll hunt thee for thy hide.
Exeunt

*Stand and fight, Greek; you are a good target.*
*No? You won't? I like your armour.*
*I'll smash it and burst all its rivets,*
*but I shall own it. Won't you wait, you animal?*
*Well then, run away; I'll seek you out in your den.*

# SCENE 7. Another part of the plain

Enter ACHILLES, with Myrmidons

ACHILLES.
Come here about me, you my Myrmidons;
Mark what I say. Attend me where I wheel;
Strike not a stroke, but keep yourselves in breath;
And when I have the bloody Hector found,
Empale him with your weapons round about;
In fellest manner execute your arms.
Follow me, sirs, and my proceedings eye.
It is decreed Hector the great must die.
Exeunt

*Gather round me, my Myrmidons;*
*pay attention. Follow my actions;*
*don't strike any blows, save your breath;*
*and when I have found bloody Hector,*
*make a fence around him with your spears;*
*use your weapons in the cruellest manner.*
*Follow me sirs, watch what I do.*
*The great Hector is fated to die.*

Enter MENELAUS and PARIS, fighting; then THERSITES

THERSITES.
The cuckold and the cuckold-maker are at it. Now, bull!
now, dog! 'Loo, Paris, 'loo! now my double-horn'd Spartan! 'loo,
Paris, 'loo! The bull has the game. Ware horns, ho!
Exeunt PARIS and MENELAUS

*The cuckold and the one who made him one are fighting. Now, bull!*
*Go, dog! Go to it, Paris! Now, my cuckolded Spartan! Go on, Paris!*
*The bull is winning. Watch out for the horns!*

Enter MARGARELON

MARGARELON.
Turn, slave, and fight.

*Turn and fight, you slave.*

THERSITES.
What art thou?

*Who are you?*

MARGARELON.
A bastard son of Priam's.

*A bastard son of Priam's.*

THERSITES.
I am a bastard too; I love bastards. I am a bastard
begot, bastard instructed, bastard in mind, bastard in valour, in
everything illegitimate. One bear will not bite another, and
wherefore should one bastard? Take heed, the quarrel's most
ominous to us: if the son of a whore fight for a whore, he tempts
judgment. Farewell, bastard.
Exit

*I am a bastard too; I love bastards. I was fathered by a bastard,*
*taught by a bastard, I'm a bastard in mind, a bastard in courage,*
*illegitimate in everything. One bear won't attack another, so*
*why would a bastard? Look out, this fight would be very*
*terrible for us: if the son of a whore fights on behalf of a whore,*
*he's risking heaven's anger. Farewell, bastard.*

MARGARELON.
The devil take thee, coward!
Exit

*Damn you, coward!*

# SCENE 8. Another part of the plain

Enter HECTOR

HECTOR.
Most putrified core so fair without,
Thy goodly armour thus hath cost thy life.
Now is my day's work done; I'll take good breath:
Rest, sword; thou hast thy fill of blood and death!
[Disarms]

*Rotten insides, so fair outside,*
*your fine armour has cost your life.*
*Now my day's work is done; I'll catch my breath:*
*rest, sword; you've had enough blood and death!*

Enter ACHILLES and his Myrmidons

ACHILLES.
Look, Hector, how the sun begins to set;
How ugly night comes breathing at his heels;
Even with the vail and dark'ning of the sun,
To close the day up, Hector's life is done.

*See, Hector, how the sun begins to set;*
*how ugly night comes creeping in on his heels;*
*as the darkness starts to cover the sun,*
*to finish the day, Hector's life is finished.*

HECTOR.
I am unarm'd; forego this vantage, Greek.

*I am unarmed; don't take advantage, Greek.*

ACHILLES.
Strike, fellows, strike; this is the man I seek.
[HECTOR falls]
So, Ilion, fall thou next! Come, Troy, sink down;
Here lies thy heart, thy sinews, and thy bone.
On, Myrmidons, and cry you an amain

'Achilles hath the mighty Hector slain.'
[A retreat sounded]
Hark! a retire upon our Grecian part.

*Strike, you men, strike; this is the man I was looking for.*
*[Hector falls]*
*So, Ilium, you fall next!Come, Troy, sink down;*
*here is your heart, your muscles and your bones.*
*Go on, you Myrmidons, and cry across the field,*
*'Achilles has killed mighty Hector!'*
*[A retreat sounds]*
*Listen!Our Greeks are retiring.*

MYRMIDON.
The Troyan trumpets sound the like, my lord.

*The Trojans are sounding the same call, my lord.*

ACHILLES.
The dragon wing of night o'erspreads the earth
And, stickler-like, the armies separates.
My half-supp'd sword, that frankly would have fed,
Pleas'd with this dainty bait, thus goes to bed.
[Sheathes his sword]
Come, tie his body to my horse's tail;
Along the field I will the Troyan trail.
Exeunt

*The dragon's wing of night spreads over the earth*
*and separates the armies like an umpire.*
*My half-fed sword, that could have eaten more,*
*is pleased with this dainty treat, and so goes to bed.*
*[Sheathes his sword]*
*Come, tie his body to my horse's tail;*
*I'll drag this Trojan around the battlefield.*

# SCENE 9. Another part of the plain

Sound retreat. Shout. Enter AGAMEMNON, AJAX, MENELAUS, NESTOR,

DIOMEDES, and the rest, marching

AGAMEMNON.
Hark! hark! what shout is this?

*Listen!Listen!What is this shouting?*

NESTOR.
Peace, drums!

*Stop the drums!*

SOLDIERS.
[Within] Achilles! Achilles! Hector's slain. Achilles!

*Achilles!Achilles!Hector's killed.Achilles!*

DIOMEDES.
The bruit is Hector's slain, and by Achilles.

*The rumour is that Hector has been killed, by Achilles.*

AJAX.
If it be so, yet bragless let it be;
Great Hector was as good a man as he.

*If it's true, there should be no bragging about it;*
*Great Hector was just as good a man as him.*

AGAMEMNON.
March patiently along. Let one be sent
To pray Achilles see us at our tent.
If in his death the gods have us befriended,
Great Troy is ours, and our sharp wars are ended.
Exeunt

*March along quietly.Let someone go*
*and ask Achilles to come to our tent.*
*If the gods have favoured us with his death,*
*we have won great Troy, and these fierce wars are over.*

# SCENE 10. Another part of the plain

Enter AENEAS, PARIS, ANTENOR, and DEIPHOBUS

AENEAS.
Stand, ho! yet are we masters of the field.
Never go home; here starve we out the night.

*Wait, there! We are still masters of the field.*
*Don't go home; we shall spend the night out here.*

Enter TROILUS

TROILUS.
Hector is slain.

*Hector has been killed.*

ALL.
Hector! The gods forbid!

*Hector! Heaven forbid!*

TROILUS.
He's dead, and at the murderer's horse's tail,
In beastly sort, dragg'd through the shameful field.
Frown on, you heavens, effect your rage with speed.
Sit, gods, upon your thrones, and smite at Troy.
I say at once let your brief plagues be mercy,
And linger not our sure destructions on.

*He's dead, and he has been dragged across the horrible*
*field in a foul way at the tail of the murderer's horse.*
*Frown on it, gods, and take quick revenge.*
*Sit on your thrones, and attack Troy.*
*I say attack us with a quick plague,*
*don't make us wait for our inevitable deaths.*

AENEAS.
My lord, you do discomfort all the host.

263

*My lord, you're unsettling the whole army.*

TROILUS.
You understand me not that tell me so.
I do not speak of flight, of fear of death,
But dare all imminence that gods and men
Address their dangers in. Hector is gone.
Who shall tell Priam so, or Hecuba?
Let him that will a screech-owl aye be call'd
Go in to Troy, and say there 'Hector's dead.'
There is a word will Priam turn to stone;
Make wells and Niobes of the maids and wives,
Cold statues of the youth; and, in a word,
Scare Troy out of itself. But, march away;
Hector is dead; there is no more to say.
Stay yet. You vile abominable tents,
Thus proudly pight upon our Phrygian plains,
Let Titan rise as early as he dare,
I'll through and through you. And, thou great-siz'd coward,
No space of earth shall sunder our two hates;
I'll haunt thee like a wicked conscience still,
That mouldeth goblins swift as frenzy's thoughts.
Strike a free march to Troy. With comfort go;
Hope of revenge shall hide our inward woe.

*If you tell me that you don't understand me.*
*I'm not talking about running away, or being scared of death,*
*but I'm daring to face all the impending dangers*
*that gods or men can give me.Hector is dead.*
*Who's going to tell Priam, or Hecuba?*
*Let the person who wants to be called a bad omen forever*
*go in to Troy, and tell them, 'Hector's dead.'*
*That is a word which will turn Priam to stone;*
*it will make springs and fountains of the girls and wives,*
*turn all the youths into statues; in a word,*
*it will scare Troy to death.But, march away;*
*Hector is dead; there is no more to say.*
*Wait.You revolting tents,*
*so arrogantly pitched on our Phyrigian plains,*
*as soon as the sun rises*
*I'll charge through the lot of you.And you, huge coward,*
*there is no space on earth wide enough to divide our mutual hatred;*
*I'll haunt you like a guilty conscience,*

*that conjures up goblins in guilty thoughts.*
*Quick march to Troy. Go happily;*
*the hope of revenge shall cover our sorrow.*

Enter PANDARUS

PANDARUS.
But hear you, hear you!

*Listen, listen!*

TROILUS.
Hence, broker-lackey. Ignominy and shame
Pursue thy life and live aye with thy name!

*Get away, you go-between servant. May disgrace and shame*
*follow you all your life, and make your name proverbial!*

Exeunt all but PANDARUS

PANDARUS.
A goodly medicine for my aching bones! world! world! thus
is the poor agent despis'd! traitors and bawds, how earnestly are
you set a work, and how ill requited! Why should our endeavour be
so lov'd, and the performance so loathed? What verse for it? What
instance for it? Let me see-
Full merrily the humble-bee doth sing
Till he hath lost his honey and his sting;
And being once subdu'd in armed trail,
Sweet honey and sweet notes together fail.
Good traders in the flesh, set this in your painted
cloths. As many as be here of pander's hall,
Your eyes, half out, weep out at Pandar's fall;
Or, if you cannot weep, yet give some groans,
Though not for me, yet for your aching bones.
Brethren and sisters of the hold-door trade,
Some two months hence my will shall here be made.
It should be now, but that my fear is this,
Some galled goose of Winchester would hiss.
Till then I'll sweat and seek about for eases,
And at that time bequeath you my diseases.
Exit

*A nice medicine for my aching bones! What a world! This*

*is how the poor helper is despised! Traitors and pimps, how they love*
*to employ you, and how poorly you are paid! Why should they love*
*our work so much, then hate us for the results? What song can describe it?*
*What example is there? Let me see:*

*The bumble bee sings happily*
*until he's lost his honey and his sting;*
*once he's lost his weapon,*
*the music and the honey are gone.*
*Good traders in the flesh, write this on your*
*wall hangings. As many of you come from Pandar's hall,*
*your failing eyes should weep at Pandar's fall;*
*or, if you can't weep, then give me some groans,*
*even if not for me, for your aching bones.*
*Brothers and sisters who guard the brothel doors,*
*Two months from now you'll see what happened here.*
*I should show you now, but I'm worried*
*that some pox-filled tart would be upset.*
*Until then I'll try and sweat to find a cure,*
*and at that time I'll pass on my diseases.*

**THE END**

Made in the USA
Monee, IL
04 March 2022